By the Grace of God

By the Grace of God

My Life as an African Bishop

Eben Kanukayi Nhiwatiwa

Abingdon Press
Nashville

BY THE GRACE OF GOD
My Life as an African Bishop

Copyright © 2024 Abingdon Press

All rights reserved.

No part of this work may be reproduced or transmitted in any form or by any means, electronic or mechanical, including photocopying and recording, or by any information storage or retrieval system, except as may be expressly permitted by the 1976 Copyright Act, the 1998 Digital Millennium Copyright Act, or in writing from the publisher. Requests for permission can be addressed to Rights and Permissions, The United Methodist Publishing House, 810 12th Avenue South, Nashville, TN 37203-4704 or e-mailed to permissions@abingdonpress.com.

ISBN 9781791033866

Library of Congress Control Number: 2024932723

Scripture quotations are taken from the Holy Bible, New Revised Standard Version, Updated Edition. Copyright © 2021 National Council of Churches of Christ in the United States of America. Used by permission. All rights reserved worldwide.

MANUFACTURED IN THE UNITED STATES OF AMERICA

CONTENTS

Preface — vii
Acknowledgments — 1

1. A Village Boy Comes of Age — 5
2. Educational Odyssey — 31
3. My Faith Journey — 49
4. In America — 65
5. Africa University Was My Crucible — 83
6. We Have an Election — 105
7. My Episcopacy — 123
8. Chabadza Partnerships — 151
9. Mukati Council of Bishops — 171
10. Leadership: A Repertoire of Skills — 183
11. Transition and Retirement — 201
12. Separation and the Future of the United Methodist Church in Africa — 215

Epilogue — 227
Notes — 229

PREFACE

There is a dearth of literature in the genre of biographies of people who end up elected as bishops of the church in Africa. This book will attempt to fill that gap. My thesis is that life-changing events in my life took place, not because of my sustained goal to pursue a certain objective, but that by the grace of God I am where I am today. Of course, I did my part by working hard, but that alone would not have uplifted me in life.

Everything that happens in one's life will have a bearing on that individual's ability to lead. I have a penchant for leadership. That does not mean that I do it well, but that I like leading when the opportunity comes. I am of the school of thought that says that one's personality and life experiences can have an impact on how one comes out as a leader. While I don't dismiss the assertion that leaders are born, I also hold the view that there is a role for attributes that can make one become readily teachable to become a leader. I have seen people who have attained higher education in leadership and related areas and yet still fail to make any headway in the field of leadership.

I hope that my story will ignite a sense of encouragement in the reader, irrespective of one's stage in life. My teaching experience at Africa University in church administration made me aware of the paucity in the availability of books on this topic. Matters related to the episcopacy should be taught in our seminaries.

ACKNOWLEDGMENTS

My acknowledgments include individuals, organizations, and experiences that initiated me into the culture of writing and publishing books. Africa University deserves a special word of thanks for opening up doors for me to enter a wider community of scholars and authors. While I was at Africa University, Dr. Ken Yamada, an Africa University and Board of Higher Education and Ministry staff member, introduced me to Professor Robert Mikio Fukada of the Doshisha University, Kyoto, Japan. Professor Fukada introduced me to the Societas Homiletica, a conference of professors of homiletics who teach at seminaries and universities. Professor Fukada went further to sponsor me to become a member of the Societas Homiletica. He also raised funds to pay for my expenses to travel and attend the conferences.

I attended my first conference in 1995 in Berlin, Germany. Pertinent to my acknowledgment is that the Societas Homiletica has the practice of assigning participants the task of writing papers, which are then presented at the conferences and published.

The next conference was set for 1997, to be held in Kyoto Japan. The theme of the conference was "Preaching as God's Mission." I read two papers at that conference: "Preaching as God's Mission: A Commentary"[1] and "Preaching Task in Zimbabwe.[2] This was my first experience of reading my papers at an international scholarly gathering. Above all, having these papers published among those of renowned professors was an awesome experience for me. At the Kyoto conference, I was elected to serve on the board, which was more of an executive committee to plan for the next conferences.[3]

I shall be forever thankful to Dr. Yamada who introduced me to Dr. Fukada. I say as well thank you to Professor Fukada for empowering me by paving the way for me to become a member of the Societas Homiletica based in Germany as its origin. I attribute the writing and publishing of this book to the initiation which I got from the Societas Homiletica. I thank all the professors who interacted with me in the Societas Homiletica at the time for providing the environment that encouraged me to write and publish this book and those I published earlier. Closer to home is the fact that one of those with whom I rubbed shoulders in the Societas Homiletica is Bishop William Willimon; neither of us were yet bishops of the church at the time.

In my family I thank Greater Taremeredzwa, who is an author in her own right, for being my constant source of inspiration at the time of writing this book. To our daughter Nyasha, I say thank you for being there whenever I needed your computer science skills as I put my material together. This was true when my wife and I visited with her in the United States for some time in May 2023 while I was working on this book.

To Pannah (Nhiwatiwa) Madzingira, who always encouraged me to put my experiences in life into a book.

To my resourceful mother, who did everything to ensure that I stayed in school during my elementary education, I say thank you, Mother. To my father, who did not use the lobola (the money exchanged for marrying one's daughter) for himself but instead kept the money safely for his son's future education. The same

Acknowledgments

father asked me, out of the blue, "Eben, what is a degree?" As I ventured to answer him, he then turned to me again in a rather firm voice, "I want you to have a degree." I can say, Dad, I got a degree and here is a book, thank you very much.

The late Professor Furusa, vice chancellor of Africa University, stood out as one who encouraged me time and again to write a book about the ways in which I was leading the church. Whenever I visited him at Africa University, we usually ended up talking about leadership.

My secretary, Rudo, did some fabulous work in handling all the technicalities of the computer. The work got easier through the help she readily rendered, as I worked on getting the book written and published.

I say thank you very much to my cabinet, clergy and the laity who worked with me in leading the church in the Zimbabwe Episcopal Area. Without them, a book like this one would not have been written.

A special word of thanks goes to my editor, Robin Pippin, whose expertise turned the manuscript into a readable book.

As the title of the book implies, I am thankful to my God for everything of significance that has happened in my life. Indeed, it is *By the Grace of God* that this book became a reality.

1

A VILLAGE BOY COMES OF AGE

Panorama View of Village Life in Africa

Sand and dust all over, cow dung in front of the house. There are no big trees, only shrubs dotted here and there. The land is nearly desert. The mountains are devoid of trees. Nowhere does one find tall grass. At evening time, darkness falls upon the village with speed and covers the sky above; everything turns into a sea of darkness. When one flies over the African continent at night, even at a low altitude, there is not even a flicker of light; it is nothing but darkness.

But if you are on the ground, you might see a bit of light from the fire in the kitchen. Usually that light dies out at about seven o'clock in the evening, that is if you are curious enough to pay attention to the time in the village. Most of the inhabitants of these households do not have enough firewood to keep the fire burning for a long time.

Where does laughter come from such darkness? Laughter is the hallmark of the African life, irrespective of the seemingly harsh life conditions. Africans laugh their lungs out over small matters such as a funny joke from a member of the family. They laugh through that darkness.

So, when I say I grew up in a village, these are some of the images my mind easily comes up with. I was born in Gandanzara village under Chief Makoni. We were a family with four children: Mary, Anne, myself, and the last born, Edson. Edson passed on when he was eighteen years of age after a long illness.

My name has a story behind it. When I was born, my parents were no longer expecting to have another child, let alone a boy. So, they gave me the name Kanukayi, which in the Shona language of Zimbabwe means surprise. When my brother John Nhiwatiwa (actually a cousin who is understood as a brother) was in school at Old Mutare Mission and heard that he had a young brother back home, he went to check for names in the school register and came across the name Eben. He liked that one. When he came home on school holiday, he told my parents that the name of the child should be Eben. My parents appreciated that new name, and it got more popular than the Kanukayi name they had given me. It was common in those days for people to have their names changed from the African name to a Western name, especially when they were baptized.

When I visited Israel some years ago, an official at the airport looked at my name in the passport. She asked me whether I knew the meaning of my name Eben in Hebrew. Although I had some idea about what the name meant, I decided that it was better to hear it from the owners of the language. So, I told her that I did not know. The officer said that it means a precious, strong stone. I liked to hear that about my name. But how did the name enter the Shona culture in Zimbabwe to the extent that my brother found it in the register of the school at Old Mutare Mission? It is not a Shona name. My assumption is that it first entered our culture through a missionary, Bishop Eben Samuel Johnson, who succeeded Bishop Hartzell as the bishop of Africa in The United Methodist Church in 1916.

Early Childhood

We were raised under a deliberate policy of being reminded, time and again, that you were either a boy or a girl. I always look at the lessons on gender equality with a critical eye. If these lessons are to make some difference, then both parents—mothers and fathers—should learn those lessons first. Culture has a tendency of instilling bad habits that become difficult to change. When we grew up, the worst thing that might happen to a boy was to cry, even if he was hurt and crying from real pain. The adult silenced you by merely reminding you that you were a man. Are you a woman? That question alone was enough for you to wipe tears dry.

The same applies to household chores: we boys just sat there waiting for the sisters to do all the household tasks. The irony of the situation is that we worked in the fields together with my sisters.

Roots

The TV drama *Roots*, based on a book by the same title by Alex Haley, was an eye-opener for many people in a number of ways. One of the impacts from the book is that a number of people became interested in their origins. We all began to think about searching for our roots. I became more aware of the information I did not have about my own roots and family. By the time the drama came on TV, I was a student at Goshen College in Goshen, Indiana. It was too late to contact elders back home to check on the details of where we came from as the Nhiwatiwa family.

The origins of my clan come from the stories that were told to us by our parents. African culture was and still is oral. Such a culture loses a lot as more adults from the earlier generation pass on.

Not long ago at a funeral in a neighbor's family on the same street where we live, I struck up a conversation with a relative of the bereaved family. When he got to know that I was a Nhiwatiwa, he asked me whether I knew a number of Nhiwatiwas that he named. I told him that I knew all of them. The good thing about the Nhiwatiwa family is that, in most cases, they have kept the family name irrespective of where he or she settled. The man mentioned something about the roots of the Nhiwatiwa family, which I had not heard before. He said that the Nhiwatiwa people originated from Swaziland under Chief Zwide. Zwide fled from the wars of Tshaka the Zulu king and went north. Later on, Zwide returned south again and finally settled in the present-day country of Swaziland.

Under the Zwide people come the cluster of the Nguni or Ngoni people and because of this connection, there are signs that there are some truths in what my friend was saying. The indicators are stories that I heard from John Rhodes Mugwambi, who married my aunt, sister to my father, a daughter of my grandfather Tendesayi Nhiwatiwa. (He got the name Rhodes because he was born and grew up during the time when the White people had entered Zimbabwe under Cecil John Rhodes.) Mr. Mugwambi used to come and visit with my father and tell some stories about my grandfather. He started those stories with, "Oh! Your grandfather, that man . . ." One I still remember is that grandfather used to come in from the fields late at night, singing a song that went like this: "*Kachi Ngoni kanoti Ntiwatiwa, Ntiwatiwa, Igwazai rombe mugwazo kuma ndege . . .*" To be honest there are some words I cannot make sense of, in either the Shona or the English language. There is a Ngoni person or Nguni who supposedly said "*Ntiwatiwa, Ntiwatiwa*" easily translated as "Nhiwatiwa. I have no idea about what "*Igwazai rombe mugwazo kuma ndege*" means.

I am confident that the *Ntiwatiwa* meant as it means today "Nhiwatiwa" because of an interesting encounter I had in Malawi. As I checked in at a hotel, the woman receptionist pronounced my last name as "Tiwatiwa" (as if the name started with a "T"). I tried to correct her that my name is pronounced Nhiwatiwa (starting with the "N" sound). She said in Malawi my name is pronounced as "Tiwatiwa." To verify her assertion, she told me that in the northern part of Malawi, which borders Mozambique, there is a white bird known by the name Tiwatiwa. What do you make of it when your grandfather is said to have sung a song with the Tiwatiwa word in it? More so that the story was told by a son-in law of my grandfather who married a sister to my father by the name Lydia. The receptionist went on to tell me that the name of the bird *Tiwatiwa* means peace. Could this be the origin of our name, which was probably popularized by my grandfather through the song he sang as he came from the fields at night? As my people mixed with other Shona people in Zimbabwe, they could not keep up with the Tiwatiwa but changed it to Nhiwatiwa, dropping the "t" and adding "nh."

What then do we say about "Kachi Ngoni"? History tells us that the Makombe tribe to which we belong settled in the northern part of Mozambique. Chief Makombe had some wars with the Portuguese who were supported by the Nguni people, who fought side by side with them. The Ngoni or Nguni came into the picture in the song my grandfather sang. The story of connections with the Nguni of Zwide could no longer be a far-fetched link back into the ancient times. History has its intrigues and puzzling issues, which could not be resolved with certainty. But even in a blanket of confusion we sometimes stumble on some truth.

My Grandfather

I cherish people and families who know their grandparents well, having lived with them under one roof. I knew my grandfather only from stories told by my father and others like Mr. Mugwambi. To make matters worse, I did not follow up to get more information. I might have asked Mr. Mugwambi more questions, but I never did. In African culture, children were not expected to raise too many questions.

On my father's side, what is not disputed is that we are of the Makombe tribe. The Makombe tribe are still found in the north central region of Tete in Mozambique. Our country of immediate origin is Mozambique. This is true of all the people of Zimbabwe; not many were born and raised here. The same applies even to Europeans—we all came from somewhere else to where we are now. If we continue to ask where the ancestors came from before Mozambique, who knows what the Zwide theory might come up with?

What pushed some of the Makombe people to flee from Mozambique were the wars they had with the Portuguese. The last Makombe king who fled from Mozambique did so in 1917 and settled in Zimbabwe, along the eastern border with Mozambique. There are a lot of the Makombe people who settled in the northeastern border between Zimbabwe and Mozambique.

Legend of Hard-Working People

Legend says that the Makombe people are a hard-working people. One writer said that one cannot find a Makombe person loitering at home. The Makombe are always found working in their fields. It is rare to see a family member loitering around the house as they will be in the field.[1] I had thought that it was just our grandfather who was known for working hard in his fields. Little did I know that this work ethic was a characteristic of the Makombe clan as a whole. The stories about how my grandfather was a hard-working man are well known in the Nhiwatiwa family.

As children we were told that there was famine in the Makoni area. The famine affected Chief Makoni himself. The chief heard that there was a bachelor, Tendesayi Nhiwatiwa, who had his grain bins full with grain. In those times tilling the fields was done by hand. To fill grain bins with corn meant that one had to work very hard indeed. An agreement was struck between Tendesayi and Chief Makoni that for a number of grain bins, Tendesayi could get the chief's daughter (my grandmother) Manakira in marriage. *Manakira* means, one who is appreciated. My grandfather was a polygamist. Grandmother Manakira was the first of the three wives of Tendesayi.

Grandfather later married two other wives from the same Makoni dynasty of the Nyati (buffalo) totem. We shall come to the tradition of totems among the some of the African people and in Zimbabwe in particular. The three wives with their husband, Tendesayi, constitute the origin of the current three Nhiwatiwa houses. We honor these houses by naming the firstborn of each of our families after the three grandmothers.

In grandmother Manakira's house was Mwarwisa as the firstborn, so we have the Mwarwisa house. In grandmother Matimbira's, the second house, we have Nyarugwe Josiah as the firstborn, so we have the Nyarugwe or Josiah house. In the third house of grandmother Pasiharigutwi, we have Richard as the firstborn, so we have the Richard house.

This is not a perfect way of keeping track of the identity of families, but we do so and it works in the Nhiwatiwa family. To check whether an event would have been well represented, one might stay with the three houses or go further to name other succeeding houses. Up to the present the Nhiwatiwa family is as inclusive in its activities as is possible. I have heard other people witnessing to the fact that we are a close-knit family when we gather for weddings or funerals. In the Bible there is talk of the twelve tribes of Israel; we the Nhiwatiwas talk modestly of the three houses of the Nhiwatiwa family.

The ethic of working hard is constantly instilled in the Nhiwatiwas. I pride myself for being born in a clan known for hard-working practices. It is a source of constant inspiration to remember how my grandfather worked hard. I would like to believe that I am a hard-working person who does not shun work. The work of a bishop is hard work, especially under the conditions we face in the African context. With such inspiration from hard work rooted in the family, that was a helpful reference point for me as I supervised the church.

Like Father, Like Son

My father not only talked about his hardworking father, he lived it. Father dug in the fields, day and night. Whenever he got out in the evening while the moon was shining, I can still hear his voice, "Why waste God's light doing nothing?" At that moment I knew that I was going to be called to do something. It was constructing a goat pen, repairing a chicken run, or digging a hole to plant some fruit trees. Whether that work was planned or not, the whole idea was to do something instead of wasting God's light.

On one of those night shifts he said that we needed to expand a goat pen. As he was putting the poles in the trench we had just dug, he asked me to hold them upright so that they would not fall. While holding those poles, I fell asleep, and one pole fell and missed him by a whisker. He asked me what had happened, and I replied that I was not able to stretch my hands to hold all of them. That was true but not the whole truth. The situation was aggravated by the fact that I fell asleep, but I not dare tell him that. Father said that next time I should use my shin to hold the poles together. Holding a line of poles with your shin is a Herculean task, but my father did not accept any reason or excuse for failing to do something. I have that same character trait of not accepting excuses for failing to implement a task. My cabinet knows that very well as we lead the church together.

Actually, when it came to working hard, all of Tendesayi's children were like that. My brother John Nhiwatiwa told me a story that happened when he himself was still a young boy. His father Thompson Nhiwatiwa was a hardworking father of ours. (In African culture, my father's brothers are my fathers, and my mother's sisters are my mothers. We don't say uncle or aunt. That is too distant.) So, Father Thompson knew that because there was a wedding going on in the village, my brother wanted to go to the wedding with other young people. His father told him that he was aware that he wanted to go to the wedding. But he also knew the reason the children want to go to these weddings: it is because they want to eat chicken and rice.

Totems

A totem is an animal or an agreed feature of creation that a clan decides to venerate as sacred. The Nhiwatiwa family belongs to the Makombe tribe, whose sacred animal is the *humba*, a wild pig or a hog. *Humba* was chosen for its power, strength, and wisdom. Those familiar with the behavior of wild animals say that a lion runs away from a wild hog. Even elephants don't come close to where wild hogs are. So, our ancestors identified themselves with the wild pig.

Usually, a clan had a way of sprucing up their totem in an embellished type of language. So we are of the *Makombe Humba, chirima nemuromo mapadza aripo, nyakupfuya* (meaning, those who plow using their mouths, leaving hoes alone, those who take care of the marginalized). Makombe actually has an exaggerated self-endowed title, implying one who covers the whole world. Lord, have mercy! These ancestors got away with anything they might have conceived. The reason someone could talk of covering the whole world is that the world they knew probably ended where the boundaries of their fields ended.

Of the Makombe Tribe

My parents and other relatives did all they could to instill in me that I was of the Makombe tribe. One cousin added some spice to it by saying that because I am a Makombe, I am therefore a *muzungu*, a bizarre accolade indeed. A *muzungu* in Shona means a White person. Why did they want to add other people so as strengthen their totem and its meaning? It so happens that when people have been defeated, the only way out as a survival tactic is to emulate your conquerors. By the time they migrated to Zimbabwe, they had already been defeated by the Portuguese and were forced to abandon their homes. When they arrived in Zimbabwe, the British were doing their thing against the Africans there. Poor Makombes, they were caught in between. So, to hold on to the belief that they were a people of consequence, I was told that I was a *muzungu*. The conqueror was a source of envy and admiration. One of my cousins with whom we share the totem went on to tell us, the young Makombes, that when we walk, we should walk upright. We look upwards. All these are not attributes of a wild hog. Walking upright and looking up is not one characteristic of which this animal is known for. We are not the only ones who identified themselves with the *muzungu*, and not all the Makombe people do that either. It was from my cousin who used such terminology. A teacher at Old Mutare Mission who came from the Eastern region where the Shangan settled used to say, *Mushangana mu yungu*, meaning the Shangan is a White person. The reasons for doing that are the same as I have explained above.

Stories from My Grandfather

Anyone familiar with the writings of former president Obama is aware of his book, *Dreams from My Father*. I have taken a leaf from that work. As I said earlier, I did not see my grandfather. What I came to know about him was a result of stories told to me, mostly by my father. One of these stories was when he called his wives and told them that he was going to fake some illness so as to expose the diviner who was extorting chickens, goats, and even cattle from people. He told them that they should call the diviner to supposedly to heal him. He went to sleep, pretending that he was seriously ill. He took a stone and put it in his mouth and pushed it to one side to create the appearance of some swelling. When the diviner was called, he, through his working tools, concluded that my grandfather was seriously ill. He touched the swollen side where the stone was and felt that it was hard. He said that in order for him to do his work well he needed to be paid a goat first. At that point my grandfather rose from where he was lying and exposed the works of this fraudulent person. The story was that the chief banished the diviner from his land.

The other story was that Grandfather did not appreciate what his mother used to do, giving his children some oil from a *mupfuta* tree. Many people in my village used the oil from that tree, believing that it had some medicinal properties to fend off illness. He was a person of his own choices and practices. He did not do things because many people did that. He went on to stop even his mother from giving her grandchildren what she believed was helpful for them. I would like to think that my great-grandmother probably gave the same oil to her son, Tendesayi.

Maternal Grandfather

If the connections of the Nhiwatiwa people with Chief Zwide of Swaziland are vague, the roots of my maternal grandfather to the Shangan people are undisputed. Soshnagana was Chief Tshaka's *induna*, or general, so to speak. He, like others, rebelled against the all-controlling rule of Tshaka and migrated north to settle in Gazaland. Gazaland straddles the eastern borders of Mozambique and Zimbabwe. Later on, the later chief well known in Zimbabwe is Gungunyana. My maternal grandparents settled in an area in Zimbabwe known as Chimanimani. The parents of my mother are known by the Ngangu surname. There is an area in Zimbabwe known by their name Ngangu. This is one of the areas which was ravaged by the cyclone Idai in 2019. Some of my relatives who were still there died in that cyclone.

At one point, White settlers demanded land and encroached in the areas where my maternal grandparents were staying. My grandparents had no choice but to leave and track inland further north and settled in the Makoni area known as Majakwara, where the remnants of the family still live to this day. By the time my father married my mother, they had already left Chimanimani to settle far from the eastern border with Mozambique.

I know very little about my maternal grandfather apart from few stories I had from his children. He was good at selecting the best soils in where to settle. He had polished up his skills in farming. He liked to grow vegetables. I also witnessed the areas he chose for his gardens. He had good milk-producing cattle. He had a habit of sending his children to learn how to work hard at a relative's farm. My family is hardworking, and they do well in food security.

The totem of my maternal grandfather and hence the one for my mother is *Chirandu, Moyo, Mukaka*. Something like, the heart, milk. The Moyo totem is highly regarded in Zimbabwe and therefore widespread.

My mother used to narrow the normally detailed explanation of the totem to *Ngorima mutsvuku,* that Ngorima, who was the chief, one who was light skin.

Maternal Grandmother

I was privileged to know my maternal grandmother reasonably well. Mother used to send me to get Grandmother to come and stay with us. I remember her as a slim woman who was strong. We walked some long distance from her home in Majakwara to Gandanzara village. As we walked, I thought that she might ask that we take a break. Instead, she was the one who used to ask me if I was still OK. Later on, I had to admit that some breaks were going to be helpful for me. So, we selected a tree with good shade, which became our traditional place to rest whenever I went to take her to our place. She liked to eat green vegetables, and I was good at growing those. I felt good when Grandmother showered me with praises in the presence of my sisters.

I like my maternal grandmother so much. She was always on my side in everything. When we were doing some work at my cousin's homestead, with whom she was staying in her old age, she was closely monitoring how much work I did each day. She did not hesitate to announce that Eben had done enough for the day. To my surprise, my cousin told me to go to Grandmother and prepare some fire for her to feel warm. That was my closing work for the day, to prepare some fire so that Grandmother was kept warm.

Early Childhood

In every culture there are patterns through which children develop. There is the usual training in doing some household chores. Then there comes a time for contributing meaningfully to the upkeep and well-being of the family. There are such duties as fetching water from the village well, gardening, plowing, and cultivating the fields. I don't want to fall into the easy but presumptuous conclusion that everything I did or that happened to me had a bearing on my future leadership. Nevertheless, there were experiences in which the village setting molded me into a capable leader.

Padare

The word *padare* in Shona has a number of meanings. First and foremost, it refers to both location and a group of people seated at that place. The word can refer to the chief's traditional court. That is the place where the chief met with his assistants to hear cases and hold trials. The sense I have in mind to which I was exposed as a young boy is different from all the above. I have in mind a place where the elders, especially fathers, gathered by the fire and visited. Such gatherings took place during the dry season and in the evening. In winter, they met around the fire to warm themselves and visit as well. The mothers prepared the meals, and we boys were sent to collect food from the different homes and bring it to the *padare*. The food was eaten communally. We children were given some morsels of the staple food *sadza*. If there was meat, the morsel was dipped into the soup and a piece of meat was also given to the child as a special treat. But the children also ate with the mothers back in the kitchen. At *padare*, the elders ate from the same plate, using their hands.

What went on at this *padare* forms the essence of this practice. *Padare* was a type of a school where we children learned about the history of the family, provided you were fortunate to have heard that type of story shared. Normally, we knew who we were as the Makombe and some details of our totem from the shared stories of *padare*.

It was also a character-shaping tradition. When I went to *padare*, I had to be prepared for character-building lessons. One day I was asked to repeat the greeting, "Good evening, Father," because I was not pronouncing the words clearly, and I was not standing in an upright position. I also needed to remember to clap hands as a sign of honoring the elders. The greeting was done one by one in the order of their birth ranking. As I said earlier, my grandfather had three wives. It was not easy to name them in their order of birth. But with time I was able to name them with ease. These activities and locations were the hub for passing on culture from one generation to the next.

Herding Cattle

Another character-forming activity was herding cattle. In Shona the question, *"Wakafudza mombe here?"*—Did you herd cattle? is a loaded question. The question is rhetorical; you don't have to give an answer. It is just a reminder that you have to behave as a tough person who has gone through it all. What happens when you are out there herding cattle could be anything hard, challenging, frightening, you name it. One thing for sure is that nothing of the sort could be reported to parents. If you report that you have been beaten, then the chances are, you will receive more bashing at home. The point is to train you to stand on your own and be able to resolve whatever challenge you might be face.

In our village we have a place we call *Mapukutu*. These are small dotted mountains with areas of both tall and short grass.

There are thickets and streams where cattle get drinking water. The grass is green. Everything is conducive for good and rich pastures.

The problem when I was growing up though, and frightening for that matter, is that dangerous and wild animals like leopards were occasionally sighted there. There were stories of such animals as lions having been seen now and then. Because the place was not frequented, the grass was tempting for one to brave out and drive the cattle out of the thickets. Adults in the village set aside days when we young ones were on school holidays to take the cattle there for grazing. They deliberately let the cattle wander into the thickets and into the dark valleys. We were then asked to go and bring out the cattle to some high and observable ground. That was the crunch of the test. The area would have supposedly been scouted for any danger; however that scouting did not guarantee complete safety for us at all. When we succeeded in herding the cattle, it was praise after praise for a job of bravery well done. We would have proven our bravery. Even as we met during the week, you were reminded that you herded cattle at Mapukutu. We were so proud of such accolades. Even to this point in time, I use the image of herding cattle at those fear-inducing places to sail through tough situations in the church. Episodes that take place during one's upbringing and related experiences coalesce to form a solid rock for reference in the future tasks of leadership. My upbringing is full of those incidences, which, upon reflection, are helpful to me.

Budding Leadership Traits

Some years ago, when I was already the bishop of the church, my sister-in-law reminded me of when I organized the Nhiwatiwa children into a so-called police force. When she mentioned that I called the children and told them that we were going to form a police force to prevent thieves from stealing our chickens, I immediately recalled the whole childish action on my part. The plan involved some training of the children in the code language they should use when they spotted a suspicious person anywhere in the vicinity of our homestead. They were to stand at strategic corners to protect the homestead. I don't remember for how long the Nhiwatiwa police force existed. All I know is that the number of chicken thefts were reduced. How much of that reduction could be attributed to the police force is hard to tell. Since these thefts took place during daylight, it might be that would-be thieves feared being spotted by the children, who knew almost everyone in the village.

After the conversation with my sister-in-law, I reflected on why she reminded me of that story at a time when the family members had come to congratulate me upon my election as the bishop of the church. I could not help but conclude that she was connecting such budding leadership traits at the time with this actual position of leadership as an adult. I am not a proponent of the theory that says leadership is a result of innate traits, and yet one cannot deny that there are nascent indicators of a leadership potential that can show in one's early childhood.

Sheer Hard Work

I grew up in an environment of hard work. There were fields to be plowed and cultivated. Firewood should be fetched near and far. Water was fetched from far away wells. This situation of fetching water from some distance has changed a bit. Some families now have borehole water at their homesteads. But not everyone is fortunate to have one. So, we walked for long distances to fetch water. Although girls did much of the fetching of water, in my family, I had to do that task. My sisters were the older ones in the family. Later on, they all got married and left me and my brother with the parents. Mother had suffered from a bout of polio when she was a child. Her right arm and leg were semi-paralyzed. She walked with a limp, but she did not complain about her disability. In most cases we forget that she had those physical constraints, but she needed help to lighten the burden.

My father liked to do all sorts of manual work. It was digging in the garden or digging holes to plant fruit trees. He enjoyed using his hands.

As I look back, I have come to appreciate my childhood, which was characterized by hard work. To this day I don't flinch from work. I see myself as a hardworking person. When I was elected as bishop of the church, I was aware that a lot of work needed to be done in the two conferences. But I felt an inward sense that I was prepared for that work.

An Extraordinary Girl Child

I call my elder sister, our firstborn in the family, an extraordinary girl child.[2] She was the epitome of the hard-work ethic to achieve what she wanted. Being a firstborn child, it dawned on her early in life that she had to take charge and do whatever was to be done. It did not matter to her whether this or that activity was "men's work," she did it. She learned how to tame oxen for use in plowing the fields. The elder brother came forward to train her in how to tame even the wildest type of oxen. She held the horns, and the ox jumped with her holding on. It was a dangerous type of work, and yet she went through it all.

Summer season was the time to plow the fields. She used to awaken the younger sister and me at three o'clock in the morning to wake up and yoke the oxen ready for plowing. The fields were some distance away from our home. We had to run to keep up with her. She needed to do that so that by the time I went to school, we would have plowed a large chunk of the fields. She practiced a type of whistling to awaken others that it was time to go to the fields. The whistling energized her to do what she was doing. By the time I was released to go to school, I was usually tired already.

There was nothing like breakfast. If I was able to get some roasted corn, the better. I put those in my pockets and ate during break at school. From the fields, we headed directly to school. We washed our feet at a stream on our way to school, yet there was no use washing because we had to walk and collect more dust sticking to our wet feet. There were no shoes to walk in. Teachers did not waste their time inspecting whether we had washed our feet. Washing or not did not make any difference. I don't know how I managed to pass examinations. Even during the exam time, we had to keep on with the same routine of waking up early. In those days school was seen as an interruption to the routine of work at home. School took children away from the tasks at home. By the grace of God, I managed to pass and proceed through the grades.

Encounter with a Hyena

My sister's display of courage could be described as reckless. At the time I grew up in our village the area was plagued with marauding hyenas, snatching goats and the other domestic animals. It was common to hear the loud noises of these hyenas even during the early hours of the evening. In fact, parents chided us for continuing to play, even when the sound of hyenas indicated that they were not far away. One day my sister heard some noise of poles being torn down by the hyena from the goat's pen. She woke up and rushed out, making all sorts of noise and sounds to frighten the hyena. The hyena ran away, leaving the goats unharmed. The following day the elders in the village chided her for such behavior, saying that what she had done was too dangerous in case it had been a lion.

Whenever I hear the word *courage*, I immediately think of my sister. She continues to be an inspiration for me. When I used to visit her at her home in our village Gandanzara, I watched her with admiration walking slowly in her old age. I would say to myself, this one at her young age walked out there in the darkness to chase a hyena! I still play around with that image in my work as the bishop of the church. I say to myself, *What can intimidate or frighten me if a hyena did not frighten my sister, this extraordinary girl child?*

Into the World

There came a time when just staying at home did not give my sister the resources she needed to improve our lifestyle as a family. Hers was an adventurous character, so she got work in Rusape, our hometown, at a brick-molding company. First my father had to give approval. Not many at that time decided to leave home and go to town for some work, especially women. The work she got was demanding in nature: molding bricks and carrying the brick forms, which were heavy in themselves.

After a few months, she came home with all sorts of utensils and other items. She really had a target when she decided to go and work away from home. She bought pots, plates, all types of silverware, and clothes for us all. I was mesmerized by some of these utensils because I had not seen any in our household as I grew up. My sister knew that her circle of friends was growing. Her friends, both women and men, were becoming regular visitors at our home and she needed some utensils to use when they visited her. It did not take long after she bought those utensils that she got married. Those utensils were used later at weddings for visitors and some dignitaries.

Impact

My sister made an obvious impact on me, even as I supervise the church. I don't claim to be doing well in the way I see women clergy. One thing is clear though, I cannot help but see women clergy though my sister. That is not fair, but that is what I do. One woman clergy said she appreciated me, saying I was doing something that the women clergy were recognizing, that is, balancing appointments of women and men as district superintendents. Actually, I don't claim that credit because the whole cabinet is supportive. I have not sensed any pushback. I am of the opinion that women clergy should be given opportunity not as a special treatment but as equals among many. My sister did everything possible for the good of our family, irrespective of her gender.

An Uncanny Love for Speaking

One of the after-hours work that young people did in the evenings was to shell groundnuts. This type of work took place a few months after harvesting the fields. My nephew, Mathias Mugwambi, and I became self-appointed village comedians to entertain people at such gatherings.[3] What we did was to imitate the missionaries and their translators. We created an unheard-of language, which we pretended to be the English language. None of us was yet able to speak English. I acted the role of the missionary who had just arrived from America. My nephew was the translator. I could just say, "*Vera mukuju* America." From that short sentence of meaningless words, my nephew chained a story that was incongruent with what would have been said in terms of length. For instance, the translation of that short sentence went like this: "I have just arrived from America. I am happy to see you. My reason for coming to this country is to preach to you so that you can know God."

The shellers did not bother that there was a disconnect with speaker and the translator. All they wanted was for the comedy to keep going, and they in turn enjoyed it. It also turned out that we pulled in a crowd, which helped the one whose nuts were being shelled. The more people, the more work was done. We were booked ahead because invitations were coming in from some distances in far corners of the village.

To this day I like speaking, not because I do it well but because that interest in speaking during my childhood got a larger part of me. In ministry and in the episcopal office, the demand for speaking now and then is obvious. Of course, we need to be engaged in listening, but to be honest here, you don't listen for long before you also want to speak. Speaking is an essential component of episcopacy.

Vital Awareness

By vital awareness, I mean the explanation which in my childhood led to the answer to a question: "Where did White people come from?" As we grew up, we saw people of a different skin color from Rusape, our nearby town, coming to our village. In most cases they came as people with authority because they came riding on horses. On a few occasions they rode on motorbikes. Elders called these the *majoni*. We have a song that the women like to sing so much in our Shona hymnbook: "*Famabnyiwo Majoni . . . Musatya mhandu dzenyu.*" This is basically translated as, "March on soldiers, don't fear your enemies, they don't have power." Still, I don't have any idea about the origin of that word *majoni*. Africans want a God who is powerful and can win over enemies. Whether the elders had in mind these horse riders when the song was sung in church, it is hard to tell.

My father's elder brother helped to unravel this enigma unknowingly, that this is where White people came from. My father's brother, Thompson Nhiwatiwa, asked that I come to his dairy in the village to help him as he was milking cows. As he was milking the cows one by one, he sang this song: "*Mombe dza baba dzakapera ne Makiwa.*" Translated into English, it means, "The cattle of my father were taken by the White people." When I returned home, I told my father about the song that Father Thompson was singing. I went on to ask what *makiwa* meant. Father said that *makiwa* meant White people. It means that White people were known by a number of different names. Father went on to tell me that there was a war that was fought in the Makoni area between the White people and the Africans. Obviously, the Africans were defeated and Chief Chingaira Makoni was executed by a firing squad.

Through reading I learned later that this war is what is known in Zimbabwe as the First War of Chimurenga. *Chimurenga* means an uprising, Africans against the colonialists. The relationship between the races was one of the defeated and the victor, with all the consequences. Things changed after the Second Chimurenga, which led to the independence of Zimbabwe in 1980.

Matters of Health

Good health is a special gift from God. I grew up with an excruciating health condition of a boil under my right ear, which was recurrent. As time went on after some treatment, it came up again in only a month or less. What bothered me was that people had to be called to pin me down so that the boil was slit open and cleaned. I hated that process of pinning me down so much that I ended up cutting the boil open myself. That did not help because it continued to come back. It was that way until my second-born sister got married and she and her husband stayed at Old Mutare Mission. My brother-in-law heard of my health condition. They arranged that if it got swollen again, I should go to Old Mutare for me to see Dr. Jane Paul Evans, who did surgery nearby. When the boil came up again, Dr. Jane examined it and then wrote a note to a doctor at the Mutare General Hospital. It was cut open without any pain because they applied some medicine that numbed the pain. But after it healed, I was instructed to come back for an operation. When I went to Mutare for a check-up, they took me into operating room. Whatever they removed, the boil has never come back again since 1961, the year of that operation.

Conclusion

My childhood experiences had a variety of leadership traits that were embedded in each and every stage of my development. My position is that leaders are born with some leadership traits that will be sharpened by training and experience. This chapter on my childhood is premised on the conviction of the existence of an eclectic view, which takes all aspects as necessary formative factors in leaders. I had no foreknowledge about where events were leading.

2

EDUCATIONAL ODYSSEY

Resourceful Mother

My mother played a critical role in my staying in school. In Zimbabwe schools require uniforms. There came a time when my father's meager salary from working at a farm was inadequate. The only clothes left for me was one set of the school uniform. To keep that uniform clean, mother had to wash it at a time when I did not have to wear clothes going anywhere. The only time for her to wash the clothes was at night.

One day she told me that I had to go to sleep early. I wanted to know why I should sleep early and leave others still playing. Mother said that it was good to obey instead of raising questions. So, I went to sleep early as she requested. When I woke up the following morning ready to go to school, I found that the uniform had been washed, ironed, and prepared. But upon wearing the clothes I could smell some smoke. Apparently, she dried the clothes over some fire. I protested that I was not going to school because the clothes smelled like smoke. She replied that as I ran to school, the wind would blow the smoke smell away.

Colonial Education

Educational rules and regulations were skewed against further studies for Africans. The government had a bottlenecked system, designed to have fewer African pupils progress through with their education. After completing elementary and primary education there was an examination meant to screen and allow only a few to progress to the next stage. Two subjects, English and Arithmetic, were essential for anyone to pass and progress. You had to get the top two grades in either subject in order to go the next step of high school. Out of a class of forty-eight pupils, only four managed to score the required grades. It was the end of education for the rest of us.

An Urge to Read

Even though I was not able to attain the required grades, an urge to read developed during my elementary education. One day as I was returning home from school, I decided to pick up some pieces of newspapers which were scattered along the road. I was not able to read any one of those pieces. When I got home tears were welling up in my eyes. My sisters asked me why I was crying. I told them that I was not able to read the pieces of the newspapers that I had picked along the road on my way home. They told me that if I kept on going to school, I was going to be able to read those pieces of paper. I then made a vow that when I got to the stage of being able to read, I would read all the pieces of papers that I found all over my village. I have developed an unquenchable appetite for reading books, which has only grown by the day all the way to the present. Indeed, reading is habit that serves everyone, but all the more so for those in positions of leadership.

Father's Interest in My Education

My father was interested in my education. It was fortunate for me to have a father who wanted me to be educated. In some cases, parents, especially fathers, quickly declared that they no longer had money to pay for their children's education. If you got enough education to enable you to read and write, that was regarded as enough. More often than not, girls were affected by this attitude. The attitude was that girls needed to read and write letters and get married. Marriage was viewed as a goal to which the girl should aspire.

When I decided to further my education through correspondence, my father was fully supportive. He had put aside some money from the lobola he got from my sisters for my education. (Lobola is the money exchanged from the groom for marrying one's daughter.) For safekeeping he gave the money to my brother John Nhiwatiwa, who was teaching at Old Mutare Mission at that time. Father agreed that I could use the money to buy some lecture notes and other required books for correspondence purposes.

Most fathers see lobola as theirs to use as they see fit. It was rare for a father to give away that money for the purposes of educating another child. There are reasons that my father was so enlightened in the area of education. During the early years, missionaries had gone out to the villages to look for children to take to the mission for school. On one of their trips to my father's village, they got interested in my father and his brothers. My grandfather told the missionary to take the elder children back to the mission but to leave my father, who was still young. The missionary insisted that even my father should also go learn at the mission. They ended up in a bit of a tug of war, the missionary holding one of Father's hands while my grandfather held the other. Somehow the missionary won, and Father went with the rest of the kids to the mission.

At Old Mutare Mission, Father herded cattle and then went to night school. He told us stories about his teacher, T. D. Kalamba, who came from Malawi. If a student failed to answer a question correctly, Mr. Kalamba began to sing a song to the tune of "Stand Up, Stand Up for Jesus." In the Shona hymnbook, the language in Zimbabwe, the song is "*Kuedza kwazosvika.*" Mr. Kalamba's song had words of his own making that, roughly translated, meant "You foolish one, you are just finishing my tea." It is interesting that Father did not tell us much about what he learned, instead he focused on the disciplinarian approach of his teacher. My father spent only a year in school. For that year he was able to write letters to his fellow pupils who were at Old Mutare at the same time with him. They understood each other's way of writing that they were taught then. The estimated year for my father's enrolment at Old Mutare Mission was 1902. Old Mutare Mission was only five years in existence counting from 1897, the year of its establishment under Bishop Joseph Crane Hartzell. This exposure to education was enough to make my father understand that education was something he wished his child to acquire.

Later on, out of nowhere, my father narrated a story of what had happened as he was visiting with others. He said the village pastor passed through where they were and decided to join them for a while. He told them that he wanted his children to go to school up to the university level and obtain degrees. Father then turned to me and looked me in the face and asked pointedly: "Eben, what is a degree?" It was difficult for me to figure out how I was going to explain what a degree is. I decided to start with what I thought he could understand. I told him that one had to finish all the stages or classes at our village school of Gandanzara. Then the person had to go to Old Mutare Mission and finish all the classes there. From Old Mutare Mission the learner had to attend school at St. Augustine Mission, which had junior college or form six by then. From St. Augustine he or she had to go to Harare to learn at a big school called the university. After four years of study if the person passed all the examinations, then one got a degree. His simple but loaded response was "I want you to get a degree." My educational odyssey had this mandate from my father that I had to obtain a degree.

Work to Supplement Income

In order to get additional income for my correspondence studies and for my general upkeep, I did some part-time work in the fields of families at the Old Mutare Mission. I made ridges and planted sweet potatoes, yams, and other crops. Sometimes it was gardening to grow vegetables. Whatever the case, I was able to get some income to meet my needs. At the same time, I decided to apply for some stable work at the Mission Farm. I got the job of herding cattle, milking them, and delivering the milk to the staff at the Mission. After skimming the milk, I loaded the cans of the milk in the bicycle basket and delivered the milk to the teachers and others at the mission. The farm manager, Denford Chimbwanda, noticed that I stayed up late. One day he came to check why the light from the candle kept on flickering late into the night. I told him I was studying through correspondence with the University of London. He encouraged me to continue studying.

Later on, the manager called me to his office and told me that he had arranged for me to go and work as caretaker or janitor at the Hartzell Central Primary School at the Mission, where there was better lighting and facilities conducive for me to study. I had done completely nothing to be able to get what I call my first promotion from a herd boy to a janitor in the midst of the Mission. There I was able to get constant inspiration by seeing students and teachers going up and down across the center of the mission. The process worked well since the elderly janitor was retiring, so I was taking his place. Mr. Chimbwanda took it upon himself to share and convince other leaders in their executive meeting that I was the appropriate person to replace the retiring janitor. I have always observed that the game-changing events in my life took place without my having made them happen. Here is such case, where a job as a janitor at the Hartzell Primary School was worked out for me and argued for in the top meeting of the leaders at the Mission, without my having applied for it. All by the grace of God.

At the primary school I worked hard under the headmaster, Mr. Mutenda, who was supportive of me. He told me to learn how to type, using the typewriter in the library of the school. In addition to work as a caretaker, I also gave out books to students who borrowed them and kept records. It was also my responsibility to supervise their general work. Students who were at the primary school at the time (1967 to 1969) called me "Brother Eben." Even as I am a bishop of the church now, members who were at that primary school occasionally still call me Brother Eben. There was that bond between us that has not faded away, even as now they have families of their own.

Epworth Theological College

I was doing well in my studies. Having passed my examination for the Rhodesia Junior Certificate (RJC), I proceeded to do my high school studies. By 1969 I had passed all the four subjects for which I had set for the examinations with the University of London. I needed to take an examination in the English language. I passed that subject while I was at the theological college (not for theological studies but continuing with caretaker work) while studying the English language in order to complete the requirements. The story of what happened after my transfer from Old Mutare Mission shall come in later chapters of this book.

A Special Visit

Rev. Dr. Maurice Culver, on staff and the representative of The United Methodist Church at the college, and the college principal, Mr. Appleyard, paid me a surprise visit in my room at the single students' quarters. My mind wandered trying to figure out why such a high-level pair of leaders at the college had come to see me. Since I was the boarding master for the single students, I figured out that maybe a student had broken one of the rules of the college, and they had come to share this news with me. But that still did not make much sense because they would have called me to the office. Instead, they posed a question of whether I wanted to go to the United States of America to study. That was unbelievable, coming to ask me whether I wanted to go to America for studies! Young people of my age at that time were always pursuing that elusive goal relentlessly without success. In my case this offer was coming to me without my having lodged any application. I told the two leaders that if it was fine with Bishop Muzorewa and his cabinet, it was fine with me to go for studies. Then they told me that they had already been with Bishop Muzorewa, who had already given a green light for me to go for further studies. In the meantime, I continued with my studies in the diploma in theology. I graduated in 1974 with an overall first position and earned a book award for the good work.

A Leaf from Bishop Cannon

In his book *A Magnificent Obsession: The Autobiography of William Ragsdale Cannon*, Bishop Cannon detailed his years of study at Yale University. He touched not only on the courses he studied but also on the individual professors with whom he interfaced. The bishop described how he remembered Professor Roland Bainton riding his bicycle to go to the library to research on Martin Luther leading to his book *Here I Stand: A Life of Martin Luther*. Bishop Cannon also makes mention of Professor Kenneth Scott Latourette who researched and wrote the book *A History of the Expansion of Christianity*. Professor Latourette produced the book by working on it one page per day before breakfast each morning.[1]

I was impressed by the way Bishop Cannon relived his relationship with his professors and the grasp he had on his subjects of study at Yale University. Some of the works he observed in the making, like the two aforementioned books, were some of the textbooks we used during my studies at Epworth Theological

College and beyond. I will use his approach as I trace my footprints in colleges and universities.

Back to Epworth Theological College

Principal Appleyard and his wife opened their home to students for dinner either as first-year students and as the graduating class. We students appreciated such hospitality from the head of the college. It was at these meals that I was introduced to foods like salad, pudding, and jelly—and also some basic table manners. From the remote village to the dinner table of a British couple was a long cultural journey.

Then we had Professor Soderstrom, a Lutheran from Sweden as our professor for philosophy and systematic theology. He taught with a permanent smile on his face. When making a point he tilted his head to one side and held his three fingers with the other hand and then delivered what he wanted to teach us. After raising a question about the existence of God, the professor began by calling my name, which he had never bothered to pronounce well. "Mr. Niyatiya, the taste of an orange is appreciated by the one who is eating it." The professor did his best to explain the connection between the eating of an orange and the existence of God. I don't think that explanation helped me very much. Instead, I relied on the traditional lessons I received as I was growing up in my village in Gandanzara: that there was *Musikavanhu*, that is, the one who created people, also known as *Chimbwe Chitedza* that one who cannot be moved, or *Ziyenda nakuenda*, that is, God without beginning or end. In fact, the whole class argued with the professor that there was no need to make arguments to prove the existence of God. At that time, we had not yet gotten to the lessons about the atheists, those who say that there is no God and don't believe in any religion.

In church history we had Professor Kare Eriksson from Norway. When I started college in 1971, Professor Eriksson taught church history in addition to leading the college as its principal. He was blind. To prepare his lessons, he enlisted his wife to read and record the elected books. When he came to teach, he did not have the tape or anything to prompt him. That was always a marvel for us. As students we struggled to remember what we saw and read with our own eyes and our professor taught us without notes. There was the professor of New Testament, Mr. Russell, from Britain. He was an excellent New Testament teacher, but I remember him most for teaching us with a cigar in his mouth. In those days there were no laws to protect nonsmokers.

Rev. Dr. Culver, from the United States, was our professor of homiletics. He had an evangelistic approach and was a great preacher himself. Dr. Culver liked to talk about the Holy Spirit, which he referred to as the *ruach* of God. His focus was that a preacher should always have *ruach* as a source of power. There was Rev. Norman Thomas who was professor of sociology of religion and Christian education. Professor Thomas also took us for practical lessons needed for the training of pastors. He created field exposure of all kinds. One I still remember was accompanying a family to search for a body of their relative in a mortuary. Our professor believed that a pastor must be able to assist the bereaved members even if it meant going into a mortuary to identify bodies. Most of us students remember him for making announcements that the motorbike which broke down last time had broken down again. He was responsible for arranging transport for students to go to some fieldwork on weekends or to go to town for some errands.

For psychology we had Professor Chigwida, who returned from his studies in the United States at the Princeton Divinity School while I was a student at Epworth Theological College. We gave him the nickname *Tambawoga*, in Shona it means one who plays alone. He was the talk of many people for marrying a White woman. We students made some bets that she was not going to make it here, given the harsh conditions and the segregation that was in Rhodesia then. On paper the law did not forbid interracial marriages, but we knew that the Rhodesian Whites gave them a hard time, especially the woman. To the surprise of everyone who had doubted, even as I write this book here in Harare, Mrs. Judith Chigwida is still here as *muroora* in the Chigwida family. *Muroora* means the daughter-in-law. In fact, they became a close mentor family for me. The day I departed Rhodesia to go to the United States, it was Professor Chigwida who drove me to the airport. When I was in the United States at the Elkhart Theological Seminary, the Chigwidas came to visit me while they were visiting the wife's parents and relatives in America. They spent two days with me at Elkhart, Indiana.

Finally, there was Professor Kurewa, the first vice chancellor of Africa University. He taught us Black theology, using as his key reference the work of James Cone, an influential American theologian. One impact of his lessons is that some of us students either scrapped our Western names or added our African ones that we had pushed into the background. That is the time when I began using my name Kanukayi over Eben.

Mennonite Biblical Seminary

Mennonite names are a bit difficult for me to remember. I found them to be different from regular American names I was used to. In any case I benefited from their emphasis on peace. I was coming from a country that was waging a war of liberation. I usually made the seminar lively by asking the professors to explain how would they have dealt with the war in Rhodesia. Professor Clarence Bowman led us in the Jesus of History Seminar. He wore a long beard. American students used to tell some of us that he was very intelligent in that he made a number of inventions. He did not talk about those inventions; instead, he drilled us on who Jesus was. The course I liked most at the Mennonite Biblical Seminary was one called the Agent of Change. With a youthful mentality, I entertained the thought that I was going to change everything upon my return home.

Goshen College

From August 1976 to July 1978, I was at Goshen College. I graduated with an Interdisciplinary Studies Degree in Political Science and Biblical Studies. The advice at home was that those of us furthering our education should branch off from theology to other courses. The idea was that we were going to lead in our mission centers as teachers and administrators. One course that had an impact on me was the one on creativity. We were encouraged to do things we had never done before. I wrote poems and expressions of creativity. Even as I lead the church, I appreciate and emphasize the need for creativity among my cabinet members. The other course was The Good Society. We read all sorts of books: *The Prince* by Machiavelli, *Utopia* by Thomas More, *Animal Farm* by George Orwell.

Illinois State University

There is a story behind my admission to Illinois State University. When I graduated from Goshen College, I started applying to universities to study for a master's degree. Each time I sent out an application, I got a reply with an offer of a partial scholarship. I just did not have any means to sponsor myself. For Illinois State, I wrote that I had no money even to buy shoelaces but what I had was the ability to study and pass my examinations with good grades. I had lost hope. Then to my surprise, I got an admission with an offer for a teaching assistantship to Professor Sessions, a professor of history in the History Department at Illinois State University. I was to maintain a B average in order to maintain the scholarship.

I got to know later on from one of the members of the scholarship committee that the way I wrote my application letter caught the attention of the committee members. A potential student writing that he had no money even to buy shoelaces was unique for them to read and led to a positive response.

Good News

On a calm fall day as I was coming out of the library, my friends Larry and Jane Matthes came to meet me. They gave me the message that my fiancée, Greater, had gotten a scholarship to come and study nursing in the United States at Winston-Salem State University in North Carolina. While I was still in Indiana, I was trying to save money for lobola to marry Greater. I succeeded in raising an acceptable amount. The transaction for the lobola took place. But the war there was raging at a heated level. She and a friend left Rhodesia for Botswana and were declared refugees under the United Nations. It was while staying in Botswana as a refugee that Greater got the Phelps-Stokes Scholarship to come to the United States to study.

When she arrived in the United States, we arranged for her to transfer to Illinois State where she was to study industrial hygiene and environmental studies. We later had our wedding while we were students there at a nearby United Methodist church. African students came from all over the United States for our wedding. When you are in a foreign land your own boundaries on the continent become meaningless, you become more of a large family. Two of our bridesmaids at the wedding were Idah from Nigeria and Caroline Manyika from Zimbabwe.

I had argued against Greater changing from nursing to the other branches of study for fear that she was not going to be able get a job when we returned home. When we did return home, Greater was one of the first women to get a degree in her area of study. She was hired by the government as an inspector of factories checking for the welfare of workers. She traveled to present papers in Sweden and met other professional women and men in her career.

Professors and Courses of Study

I studied history under Professor Haddad. He introduced me to seminars in history where I was exposed to the technical methods of research. My understanding of the methods and the study of history matured.

At the doctoral level I studied under Professor Kyle Sessions, for whom I was a teaching assistant. He was thorough and rigorous in his demands for further reading and research. I came out of his courses with a feeling of having been well educated in my area of study.

University of Zimbabwe

In Zimbabwe it was a requirement that you had to have teaching experience if you were to teach in any way. I was teaching at the high school at the junior college level, form six, including other pastoral activities, but teacher training was required even for those with degrees. I had to take the Graduate Certificate in Education at the University of Zimbabwe. I enrolled as a part-time student while at the same time teaching my classes at Old Mutare Mission. The professors had to assess my practical work from what I was teaching in my classes. I passed my examination both practical and written with merit. Merit is a high-level grade at the University of Zimbabwe.

My training in teaching became handy upon assuming the role of the episcopacy. Teaching is commonplace for bishops. I instituted what I called the Bishop's Mobile College. I went out into districts to teach on various topics. I used my training to enhance my delivery abilities. From Professor Sessions I had learned about what he merely called the "List of Terms." I use that approach more often than not when I present my lessons.

Emory University

My educational odyssey took me to Candler School of Theology, Emory University in Atlanta, Georgia. I took a break from Africa University to take up a staff development program. From 1995 to 1996 I was enrolled in a master's in theology program. I had also hoped to study preaching under Professor Fred Craddock. Unfortunately for me, Professor Craddock had retired by the time I got to Candler. I then studied homiletics under Professor Kyser. He introduced me, among other areas of study, to homiletical resources. The gist of the course was that a preacher should be on the lookout for possible material that might be used in preaching. One of the spellbinding types of books he had the class read was *Saint Paul at the Movies*. Back at Africa University, I introduced Homiletical Resources as a new course of study with the approval of Professor David Kekumba Yemba (now Bishop Yemba).

Another area of interest for me at Candler was the focus on contextual theology. Everything must be viewed within a given context. Finally, there was a course in church administration taught by Bishop James Thomas. What a humorous bishop and professor he was! Bishop Thomas taught us in an area I now know as self-care. He said that when preparing a diary or calendar, a pastor should have areas marked "SWW," meaning, shopping with my wife. Even if the diary is picked up by someone, they will think that it is marked for a very important meeting. As students of his class in that course, we made a booklet of a collection of his sayings and presented it to him as a surprise gift to say thank you very much for the course. I misplaced my booklet, and I always wonder if I could somehow get a copy of that booklet from one of those students.

Conclusion

My educational journey was long and meandering. There were a lot of constraints and hurdles to be overcome. On the other hand, God was always ahead of me, resolving some of the bigger challenges. For that I shall forever be thankful. It is within this educational odyssey that I see the hand of God. God's grace was overflowing when Principal Appleyard and Professor Culver came to my room to ask whether I wanted to go to America to study. My cup of grace was spilling over when my fiancée managed to secure a scholarship to join me in our further studies and marriage in America. God was still not done with me when I got a scholarship to study at Illinois State University because of an application letter that sounded unusual.

3

MY FAITH JOURNEY

Understanding the Term

It was in the Council of Bishops that I heard the term "faith journey" for the first time. Of course, I knew of terms like "spiritual pilgrimage" or St. Augustine's *Confessions*. The practice of sharing one's faith journey is integral to the activities of the Council of Bishops. I looked forward to the time when bishops shared their faith journeys. It was not clear whether every bishop had an opportunity to share his or her faith journey. That act of grace skipped me. I did not have the opportunity to share my faith journey.

But even as I write this book, I am still not clear about what the core of a faith journey for a bishop should be. Is one's faith journey in the Council of Bishops about one's call to ministry? Or is faith journey in the council a look back and trying to make sense about how on earth one became elected to the episcopacy? Or is the faith journey about the general spiritual development an individual has gone through?

For me, the faith journey is contextual. I assess and understand my faith journey in the context of African spirituality. Whatever the answers might be to the questions which I have raised earlier, there will be no comprehensive understanding of my faith journey without embracing African spirituality. In the African context, spirituality is an integral part of the whole life. Life is lived as a holistic entity, including its spiritual component. When I grew up in the village, any adult could admonish me from certain behaviors. I was guided to follow a specific faith journey, so to speak. When adults chided us young people for sitting at the intersections of the road, they said it was to prevent the illness of having boils all over our bodies. The truth of the matter was to stop us from being run over by a car or truck. These teachings came packed in some form of belief. The faith journey entails the ability to go beyond these superfluous beliefs and understand the essence of such teaching.

The faith journey in an African culture was embedded in the fables that the parents shared in the evenings after meals. Most if not all of the fables had some moral teaching. An example is a fable in which some hare invited the baboons to a party. In order to eat the meal and enjoy the party, everyone had to wash hands first at a nearby stream just before getting to the place where the hare lived. The hare burned the grass around the rock where the party was going to take place. On their way to the party the baboons washed their hands, but they still had to walk over the burnt grass and got their hands dirty again. When they arrived, the hare checked whether the hands of the baboons were clean. Of course, they were dirty, so they had to go back and wash again. The process went on and on until the party had finished without the baboons participating.

The moral of the story is to show how cruel and cunning the hare were by ill-treating the baboons. The baboons were a laughing stock. It is not good for us humans to cheat others like that. As young people we got the point and sympathized with the baboons and hated the hare. We vowed not to behave like that to others as we grew up. There is no biblical reference or a pastor as an intermediary. So is this a valid component for a faith journey. The source for moral teaching for the Africans was the whole environment and not a certain segment of it.

Parental Role

Father

My father had no direct role in my faith journey, that is, if we view faith journey as a process limited to what one gets in the context of a Christian church and its religious connections. What I got from my father was what I call the faith in the past tense. The stories of faith I heard from my father were his past experiences. He talked about the missionaries who took him from home to go to Old Mutare Mission. The one year he spent at Old Mutare Mission in school exposed him to some Christian teaching. Father used to sing some songs they were taught at the mission. It was not clear whether he really wanted us to learn to sing the way he did or whether it was a way of letting us know that he had some idea about the teachings of the church.

Back home in Gandanzara, he went to church under Pastor Benjamin Katsidzira. He did not talk about what he learned in particular. Instead, he talked about how naughty his young brother Maziwangeyi and his friend were, coming to church late so that they disturbed the people as they entered during the time of prayer. They put some nails under their shoes so that they made some noise upon entering the church. They enjoyed being chased away.

Within the family, Father did not show any interest in encouraging us to worship God. When we held evening prayers, which my mother organized and encouraged us to do, Father was disinterested. Each time mother talked about evening prayer, he talked about frightening stories of the possibility of being dragged out by a lion while eyes were closed in prayer. It was not fun at all because I developed a habit of closing one eye while keeping the other open to watch for lions. For a father to tell stories of lions dragging us children during prayer was hindering our faith development.

It was possible that my father was baptized when he was still a child, probably at the time he went to Old Mutare Mission. His names tell the story. His Shona name was *Chatendwachinyi*, meaning, what can you thank them for. But he also had the English name—William, not a biblical name. Southern Rhodesia being a British colony, maybe someone heard of the British Monarch William and grabbed that name and dumped it on my father. Another puzzle is that the grave of my grandfather was near the old village church at a place they were settled before moving to the present village of Gandanzara. Usually, missionaries did not allow someone unconverted to be buried near the church unless that person had some connection with the church. But my grandfather's name was the sweet Shona name Tendesayi that means, be thankful.

The only positive contribution to my faith journey that Father made was the story he told me about how Grandfather exposed a cheating traditional healer, which I narrated in chapter 1. My father used that story to teach me that I should shun witch doctors in my life. He emphasized that darkness will attract darkness. The best way is to stay out of such beliefs. Simply put, a life in which one relies on magic leads to a world of deceit. I have held on to that teaching firmly to this day.

My Mother

My mother had a direct and rewarding impact on my faith journey. Mother was a full member of the church. She was a member of the women's organization called the *Rukwadzano Rwe Wadzimai*, or RRW. Worship in The United Methodist Church in Zimbabwe is anchored in the women's organization. The women were the center of focus at the ten-day camp meeting revivals. These camp meetings usually took place during the month of September, when schools closed for holidays. My mother asked me to accompany her to the camp meeting to fetch firewood and water. She did not emphasize the spiritual benefits to me for attending those revivals. So, I did accompany my mother, thinking more about helping to fetch water and firewood, and above that, the idea of playing with friends.

At the camp meeting, we children were grouped together and had teachers to guide and teach us Bible verses. Among other things, we were taught songs and memorized Bible verses. We did some drama based on a story in the Bible. It turned out that we learned far more at these camp meetings than I would have imagined. When you add these experiences to the Bible lessons we got at school, the learning process was rich. We ended up with a full kit of knowledge about the Christian faith, which sustained our faith journeys.

When I was in my teens, I became a member of the United Methodist Youth Fellowship. This group was active at the camp meetings. We were given opportunity to make presentations of reciting Bible verses or give some testimonies about what we were learning. These camp meetings were influential in shaping my spiritual formation.

Village Pastor

Our village pastor, Rev. Patrick Machiri, was very visible in the village. I remember Reverend Machiri as one who wore oversize suits, and I later figured out why. The missionaries brought used clothes and gave them to pastors without regard to the sizes. The notable factor was that most pastors were older. Most of the pastors joined ministry after having served in some other careers. So, they came to ministry after spending their young years in the other fields of choice. Most would have served as teachers or nurses. Anyway, he looked old to me.

Reverend Machiri was a regular visitor in people's houses. As I came to know later, the pastor was making pastoral visitations. As children, we imitated the way he walked in slowly measured steps. We concluded that walking slowly and in fact being slow in everything was the hallmark of sainthood. It was the way of the holy people of God, so we thought. With the exception of one thing, we children had no problem with our pastor. That one thing was forbidding us from playing a game of soccer, kicking our plastic ball on Sundays after church. The pastor's understanding of the Sabbath as a day of rest meant that even for us children, playing with that plastic ball on Sundays was disobedience to God. One Sunday, unbeknownst to us, the pastor passed through where we were playing with our plastic ball. He picked up the ball and emphasized that we should keep the Sabbath day as a day of rest. He then went away with our ball. As a way of revenge, we decided to nickname the pastor "*ka* god." *Ka* denotes small. Therefore "*ka* god" means "a little god" with the small letter "g." We made sure that we were not going to give the pastor the status of God. Our issues with the pastor meant that the faith journey became distorted, not because the pastor did anything really wrong, but because we were still too young to comprehend the meaning of Sabbath, beyond the fact that the Sabbath was not good for us.

Making children interested in what goes on in an adult Sunday worship service is an uphill task. It was more so for us attending services with no children's stories, and we were expected to sit through a three-hour service quietly. The most boring time, when I wished I were anywhere else but church was when the congregation sang the song "Holy, Holy, Holy." This sounded so dull and boring to me. It was later in my understanding that I came to realize that the song grounded worshippers into the theology of the Trinity. In fact, I had an inquisitive mind and wondered why church songs were not as exciting as those sung at weddings. Indeed, before my time of understanding such complex issues, I was already searching for answers about why songs at church did not interweave cultural norms in them. I merely dismissed those questions by concluding that things of God were naturally boring. Of course, this was a childish conclusion.

Old Mutare Mission

During my time of staying at Old Mutare Mission while doing my studies through correspondence was also a time of spiritual growth for me. Old Mutare Mission is known within United Methodist Church circles as the *manyuko*, that is the fountain, or where the church started.[1] Some of us young men who were working in different departments formed our own "Holy Club," based on the little knowledge we gathered about John Wesley's Holy Club at the University of Oxford. We made vows that we were committed to a life of prayer and to living a life of obedience to God. We also attended the sunrise services organized by the women's organization on Sundays. These sunrise services are called *Rumuko*, that is, to rise. Rumuko was critical in cultivating my faith journey.[2]

While still at Old Mutare Mission, attending camp meetings had become my way of life. In 1968, I attended the camp meeting at Chiringa Odzi. I had a strong feeling within me that I had to commit my life to Jesus Christ as my Lord and Savior. I responded to the altar call and testified that I had received Jesus Christ as my personal Savior. From that point onward, I felt an abundant freedom to express my Christian faith at will. I was ready and willing to accept tasks in the church.

I became the Sunday school teacher for high school students who were preparing to be baptized. Later on, I became a local preacher under the mentoring of David Maenzanise in the surrounding farms. That was also the time of my evangelical inclination in spreading the gospel in the surrounding areas to bring people to Christ.

Call to Ministry

My call to ministry took an indirect way. When the Board on Ordained Ministry interviewed me at Old Mutare Mission in 1969, I was not yet clear about how God had called me to ministry. It was after I had already become a pastor that it became clear how it all happened. Although I had satisfied the board in viewing me as a potential candidate for ministerial training, I gave them a different narrative.

Taking up ministry as a career is associated with a response to the call from God. This tradition is well established in The United Methodist Church. I trace my call to ministry to my childhood days. The main source for my spiritual nudges to become a minister of religion was my village pastor. I used to engage in a silent personal dialogue within myself. Each time I saw Reverend Machiri making his pastoral visits in the village or in the church, I mused that if I knew of anyone who aspired to become a pastor, I would have told him or her to do it without delay.

My reference to the choice of a young person came from the fact that our village pastor was in his old age. I was looking for one who would have opted to become a pastor while still young at our village clinic at Rugoyi. I even hoped that such a young person would have been well groomed by wearing well-fitting clothes as our teachers did. The fact that the oversized suits were donations that the missionaries brought from their home countries was oblivious to me at the time.

Little did I perceive that I was the young person I was imaginarily looking for. However, this is not the story that I told the Board of Ordained Ministry when they interviewed me at Old Mutare Mission. It became clear to me as I reflected later in my ministry that this was the way God called me for God's service. The role of my village pastor became so prominent in my call to ministry.

Actually, other pastors also are a part of my call to ministry. I have already alluded to how the pastor and the leaders at Old Mutare Mission gave me responsibilities to do church work, such as local preacher, Sunday school teacher, and other roles. One day our pastor at old Mutare Mission, Rev. David Mudzengerere, came to where I was doing some work watering flowers at the Hartzell Primary School. He asked whether I wanted to preach in the Ehnes Memorial Church on the following Sunday. My response was a yes. But after sharing the news with friends that evening, my friends thought that it was foolish for me to have accepted the invitation to preach. What was I going to say before a congregation of high school students and their degreed teachers? Yet, some friends encouraged me to go ahead and preach, always relying on God.

I took the text of my sermon from where Jesus admonished the crowds that they should not be like graves that are painted white and yet inside there are only skeletons (Matt. 23:27). At the end of the service Reverend Mudzengerere called me to his office. I thought the pastor was going to scold me for castigating the congregation with my sermon. The pastor went straight to the question. He wanted to know whether I wanted to become a pastor of the church. My response was a yes. The process to go through the required stages started immediately. In 1969 I went before the Board of Ordained Ministry. The outcome was that I was going to transfer from Old Mutare Mission and go to Epworth Theological College effective January 1, 1970. I was going to continue working as a janitor while I continued to study my English language. They wanted me to proceed to the diploma level, which required a high school certificate. The projection was that I was going to pass my English language requirement in 1970 and then proceed to begin theological studies in 1971. Although I accepted the arrangement, deep down I was complaining that they should have let me begin my studies without any delay.

On reflecting upon all these decisions by the church leaders, I now know that they were operating at a higher level of wisdom than I grasped at the time. The plan worked well, as per their projections. I passed my English language requirement and started my theological training in January 1971. At Epworth Theological College I spent most of the time working at the office of the principal, Rev. Kare Eriksson. I continued with my work as a janitor. Reverend Eriksson was blind, but as he sat at his desk, I always had this strange feeling he was seeing me. I did my work to the best of my ability.

Spiritual Formation at Epworth

Epworth Theological College was a rich environment for United Methodist students. We had a spiritual formation group for both single and married students. We met once a week for a time of sharing, study, preaching, and prayer. Everyone had an opportunity to share joys and challenges. At times we studied selected chapters of a book in the Bible. I looked forward to those meetings, which were truly nurturing as we shared among ourselves as students. Another spiritual formation component was the Wednesday chapel services. The Wednesday morning services were mainly for students and staff. Those services also served as the practical platform through which the students were assessed. Sunday evening services were for the whole college community. Such an exposure to matters of worship and general spirituality was enriching.

In Harare as part of the college curriculum all students were attached to a congregation. At those congregations, tasks included but were not limited to preaching, teaching Sunday school, and leading the children's Sunday school. Later, when I taught at Africa University, Bishop David Kekumba Yemba, dean of the Faculty of Theology, requested that I teach spiritual formation to all theology students. I accepted with joy.

These are brief examples of the rich background that I had about how spiritual formation events can be of tremendous help in spiritual development. Even in my position as the bishop of the church, I am interested to know whether sections are meeting and strengthened. These small group meetings are the bond that binds the church together.

Geographical areas of the circuit are divided into sections. Each section has its own leader for a group of about five families. The section leader is constantly connected to the pastor and the other church leaders in a two-way communication system. One can say that the Zimbabwe Episcopal Area experience with sections is a replica of class meetings in the long heritage of the denomination.

Life of Prayer

I believe in a life of prayer. I have developed a sense that when I pray, God is by my side, physically. The first day of classes at Epworth Theological College, I knelt in my room and made a covenant with God in prayer. I thanked God for taking me that far in my life. I made a request to God to open my mind in my studies at the college and beyond.

In the same vein, when I arrived in the United States in Akron, Pennsylvania, I requested to be taken to a church and was taken to a Lutheran church. I entered the church and offered a prayer of thanksgiving. I thanked God for the safe journey but

I mainly requested that I keep focused on what I had come to America to do.

I found the United States of America to be overwhelmingly big in every way. Mr. Hodzi, a teacher at Hartzell High School, had just returned from the United States. He had given me a brief but helpful orientation about America. He told me that America was a big country, and everything in it was big. Mr. Hodzi was correct in his assessment of how awesome the United States of America is. Even though I have visited America many times now, the overwhelming sense of bigness still remains with me each time I visit. In his orientation to me, Mr. Hodzi concluded by urging me to remain focused because, for many reasons, it was easy to lose track in the United States.

I therefore prayed in that church on my first day in America that like the man in the parable holding on to a plow, I should never look back and away from my studies. As I rose from the altar I had this sense of spiritual fulfillment beyond what words might be able to explain.

The World of Demons

When the Bible talks of demons, it is referring to the world that is still so close to the spiritual experiences of Africans in a different context. My spiritual journey led me to scenes where I witnessed the elders, both laity and clergy, exorcising demons from people who were possessed. Sometimes a song was sung, with hands laid on the head of the possessed. The one with the demon might speak out saying who he or she is in the spirit world. These demons were given names depending on what behavior they induced in the possessed person. For instance, if the demon made someone to climb up the tree, then the demon was of a baboon. Other demons claimed that they had traveled a long distance, searching for the person they wanted to possess. Sometimes, when a Bible was put on the head of the possessed, the person then shouted back that he or she was being burned.

It is common to hear pastors giving testimonies about how they encountered demon possession of people in their pastoral experiences. These days there are fewer instances than was the case in the past. This underworld of demons is complex even for the African people. Is it just something reflecting multiple personality disorder, or is there something more to it? These are questions that have no easy answers.

I have had a personal encounter with this spirit world. This one was with someone who had hired a maid to help him. The male person was single. One night, there was some noise at the house of that person. People came to wake me up. When we got there, we found the woman scantily dressed, seated on the floor. The man was in the corner inside the house. The woman kept on talking in a voice that sounded like the voice of a man speaking through her. Through that voice she was speaking in a third person. The man speaking through her castigated the man in the corner, that he was like a snake that bites what it does not eat. The voice said that he (the one speaking) had traveled a long distance looking for "my bag." Demons call the people they possess, "a bag," to live in. In the meantime, we continued singing hymns from our church hymnal. We dialogued with the demon, asking him to leave the woman alone and to go back to where the demon had come from. After some time and prayer for the demon to depart, the woman finally came back to her senses.

Afterward, we asked her what had happened. She said that the man had proposed that they enter into an intimate relationship, and she had agreed. Then they went to retire for the night, and from that point on, she did not remember anything until the point when we were there in that house. We then asked whether she had anything to say about the whole episode. She said that she had a demon that did not want her to be married. Each time she entered into a love relationship, the demon attacked her so as to break up the relationship. She said she did not want to live under the spell of the demon any longer. She pleaded for prayers to be offered so that she might be cleansed from the demon. We offered prayers. We then instructed that they terminate the contract for the cleaning job and that she return to her family. The following day she left and returned to her parents.

Other cultures, especially the Western culture, get puzzled by stories of the spirit world. But in the African context, a pastor might as well expect such a scenario to come up during the time of one's ministry. Our theological training does not say much about these spiritual issues. The best thing a pastor could do is to express sincere and convincing faith to pray for the demons to leave people free from bondage.

Conclusion

Spirituality is made up of so many things: images, sounds, feelings, visuals, words, and tastes. Each time I reflect on matters of my spiritual journey, the experience which I had at the airport in Zimbabwe in August 1975 on my departure day for the United States comes up vividly on my mind. Family members including my mother and brother John Nhiwatiwa, my professor Max

Chigwida, and Mr. and Mrs. Rukunda gave me a resounding sendoff. The airport had a balcony, which made it possible for people to get up on the platform and be able to see and wave goodbye to those beloved ones departing. In my case they sang a Shona song, *"Fambayi na Jesu pa Nzira Dzese"* meaning "Travel with Jesus in all your ways." I kept on hearing the song till the door of the plane was shut for takeoff. The sound continued to come in my mind long after the plane was in the air. It was only when I knelt at the altar in that church in Akron, Pennsylvania, and proclaimed Amen at the end of the prayer, that there was closure to my sendoff at the airport in Harare, Zimbabwe.

4

IN AMERICA

Writing about the culture of other countries is not easy, even more true when writing about such a big country as the United States of America. Listening and learning from the Americans themselves, I came to understand that they have what may be called regional cultures. For those of us visiting from other countries, even for a long time, it takes time to identify these differences. More often than not, we do not understand it without some explanation to make things clear. There is the southern culture, the northern culture (or cultures), and many more.

The parameters for this chapter are impressions I received from personal encounters and experiences. The United States is known and talked about by many people around the world, including those who have not been there. Its culture is on display on television screens in many countries. Young people from other countries aspire to go to the United States, even more than they openly admit. On one occasion when I was also applying for my visa to visit the United States, I sat next to the window where some young people were being interviewed. I could not help but hear part of the interview. The embassy staff asked the young person why not apply to go to the University of Zimbabwe. I knew that the young person wanted a student visa to go and study in America. I did not hear the response that the young person gave, but I could bet that there were some creative ways of trying to convince the embassy staff for a visa.

People see America in different ways. In this chapter are my own impressions, which I do not claim to be representative views of others in any way.

Observations from Returnees

In Zimbabwe we have had many people go to study in America for many years. When they returned home, we heard some strange stories about their behavior. We heard that some of them claimed to would have forgotten what a goat was called in the Shona language that is spoken in Zimbabwe. In other words, they gave the impression that they had forgotten the Shona language. The same applied to food: some returnees told their parents and relatives that they did not eat *sadza* anymore. *Sadza* is a staple food in Zimbabwe made from cornmeal in the form of grits or thick porridge. They gave the impression that America is a country that makes one forget his or her own language and culture. As many could also testify, I did not have any challenge of forgetting my language, even after staying in America for many years during my studies.

Orientation

Before I came to America in August 1975, I already had some indirect preliminary orientation. Now and then, one could observe and learn something about America from the missionaries.

Unfortunately, American missionaries rarely invited Africans into their homes. I have already given an example of invitations we received from our principal at Epworth Theological College to his home. But he was not American; he came from Britain. Invitations also came from Mr. and Mrs. Eriksson, who came from Norway. In any case we learned a little bit whenever we got a rare invitation from our American missionaries. Unfortunately, American missionaries did not talk about their home countries, whether in class or in any other setting. Instead, they liked to talk about the host countries.

Missionaries always seemed conflicted about how to behave as they related to the Africans. Later, we came to understand that American missionaries were coming from a country where relations between Blacks and Whites were strained. Yet they were taking vows to work and uplift the Black people on the continent of Africa. At the same time, they projected a sense that, in working among the Africans, they were sacrificing. Well, sacrifice they did for sure, but this had to be put in context. Missionaries did everything to hide from Africans that they were actually "working" as missionaries to earn their living. This situation put them in an awkward position, which led them to avoid talking about their home country in a way that would have made it clear to the Africans that their home country had a "good life" beyond what words could express. Instead of showing pictures about how Americans lived, they took pictures of the deplorable conditions that they encountered in Africa and showed those photos back home. Maybe they had no choice but to show those conditions so as to induce sympathy and raise funds from the home country.

Things have changed through protective laws that prohibit photographing people without their consent. This is more so for children, who need such protection the most. I learned little or close to nothing about America from some of the missionaries who served in Africa. Let me hasten to say, though, that I stayed with a missionary couple when I had my study time at Candler School of Theology at Emory University. So, I don't want to give the impression that missionaries did not ever open their homes to the African people.

Films

Films were a powerful and influential form of communication that could give wrong impressions. The Tarzan-type of films gave a distorted picture of how Africans lived. We saw movies of Tarzan jumping from one branch of tree to another in the jungles. We always wondered where they were getting such people living in trees, since our villages were almost desert from deforestation.

A different approach came with arrival of a young man who came as a missionary at Old Mutare Mission. Ted DeWolf arrived at Old Mutare Mission in 1968. He quickly made friends with the Africans who were also teaching at Hartzell High School. He introduced a program of entertaining students with films shown in the evenings. I remember one show that I attended featuring Elvis Presley. That was an eye-opener for me and others! We were exposed to an area of the American culture through music. When I got to the United States and got to know of other musicians such as Dolly Parton and other singers, that Presley film show had prepared me. A visit to the Country Music Hall of Fame in Nashville further exposed me to music in the United States. Mr. DeWolf married a daughter of a missionary, Shirley Culver. Her father, Professor Culver, taught me preaching at Mutare Mission. Shirley's uncle, Professor Marshall Murphree, a son of an early missionary to Zimbabwe, lived in Zimbabwe with his wife till death and were buried in Nyanga.

Orientation from Mr. Hodzi

One of my most helpful orientations before leaving for America was from Mr. Hodzi, who had just returned from America when he came to teach at the Hartzell High School. When he arrived at Old Mutare Mission, I was preparing to leave for studies in America. I took the opportunity to visit with him whenever time permitted to learn about America. At that time I was an assistant Bible knowledge teacher. I was also a chaplain at the school and had easy access to talk to Mr. Hodzi. He went on to advise me that it was possible for one to be overwhelmed by everything in America and forget what you were there for. Mr. Hodzi gave me his camera to take pictures, which came in handy when making presentations at gatherings. He also told me that it would be helpful to buy a handbook about Zimbabwe so that I could use to show people places of interest in the country. As it turned out Mr. Hodzi's orientation was helpful in ways I would have not have imagined.[1]

Upon Arrival in the United States

When I arrived in the United States, the port of entry was JFK International Airport in New York. Getting a bird's-eye view from the plane as it descended, I had an overwhelming sense of awe. It was awesome to see the expansive terrain covered by New York City.

Irrespective of how many times I have been in the United States, this feeling that it is an awesome country stays with me. Americans are rightly proud of their country. More times than not, I have been asked whether I have been to America before. I noticed that if I say oh, yes, I have been to America before, people feel at a loss as to what to say next. But those very first years when my answer was it was my first time to be in the United States of America there was some jovial readiness to share more. I think that Americans are aware that first-time visitors to their country feel a sense of being overwhelmed by almost anything. I don't ever ask whether someone has been to Zimbabwe before. It is not that I am not proud of my country; the reason is that I think of Zimbabwe as one of the many countries on this planet—nothing more, nothing less. Whether someone has been to Zimbabwe or not is no big deal.

Another question that Americans seem oblivious about is when they ask us the question: "When are going back home?" To an African like me, that question is both annoying and embarrassing. In African culture it is impolite to ask your guest when he or she is going to return home, whereas Americans find it polite to ask about your journey, think that traveling is tiring, and assume you are eager to return home.

Meal at the Church

My first meal at a gathering was at a church, after the worship services. To understand the level of my shock and surprise, allow me to walk the reader briefly through the culture of food I came from in my home country. The staple food in Zimbabwe is *sadza*, which I have already referred to earlier. *Sadza* goes with other food, what we call relish, which can be vegetables, meat, beans, or something else. In fact, *sadza* is so important to us that my mother's first concern was what I was going to eat in the far country to which I was going. Deep down I also shared her worry because I was not sure how I was going to survive without *sadza*. My mother convinced me to pack some cornmeal so as to prepare *sadza* in America. Then the next question was, how much should I pack to last me for long time there? Thank God that now you can go the nearest market and get all sorts of food items from around the world, including the right cornmeal to prepare *sadza*. But when I got to the United States in 1975, we had to rely on grits and mix it with flour to come closer to prepared *sadza*.

Back to the meal at the church. The table was full of food from corner to corner. With all that food, I did not see sadza. That means that for me there was no food. There were all types of meat, fish, beef, pork, and chicken. I recognized salad from the experience of having meals in the principal's house while I was a student at Epworth Theological College. Vegetables, some kind of starch, desserts, and sweets occupied other corners of the table. Problems come in different packages. My problem was to sort out what was real food to take the place of *sadza* and what was relish. Should I choose to take chicken and stay with it, or fish, or mix? To honor me as the guest, the servers wanted me to go first. I wanted to be rescued by first observing what the rest were doing, but I went ahead and picked some baked potato and fish. Someone who was observing what I was doing noticed that I was about to leave the table. He asked me whether I didn't enjoy the rest of the food. I had to be honest and tell him that I thought I had to select only one of each food item. The explanation was given that I had to take and sample anything at the table, as long as I still had the appetite to eat. I could not believe what I was hearing. At home the issue of relish was a big one. A chicken must be eaten for more than two or three days in the family. This was an important encounter with America for me. If you don't have limits for food, then you surely don't have any problem on this earth, so I thought.

There was also the concept of the "free refill." This one I encountered in the fast-food restaurants as a student, where we got most of our lunches and dinners. I was surprised to find that if you finished your first glass of soft drink, you could go back and have it refilled without paying any more money. I had heard that America is a land of plenty. In America, you don't eat only because you are hungry; you eat because it is nice to enjoy the process of eating and also the place where you want to go and have your meal. Related to the experience of the meal at the church is the observation that America is a land of choices. Having choices is the hallmark of American culture. In America, failure to have choice is as if someone is taking away your freedom.

Thank You

The words "Thank you" should be on your lips if you ever plan a visit to the United States. Of course, all people want to be thanked for something they have given or done. But this is different in some instances in the African culture. African culture has some sense of entitlement: you are my son or daughter and I am your father or mother or a relative, so you have to do that for me. If you are not so fortunate after giving them something, they will immediately make a list of items that you should bring next time—even without having thanked you for what you would have already done. I want to believe that I am doing better now in remembering to express sincere thanks to Americans. Even in Africa, we appreciate a word of thanks so that people won't think that things are given to them as a right. You have to express some thanks. There is a colleague bishop with whom the Zimbabwe Area has been in partnership. He had mastered the Shona word for thank you, which is *mazvita*. I noticed that those in Zimbabwe who received those expressions of thanks appreciated that. True to the word, every culture welcomes a word of thanks.

Easy Access to Facilities

In America facilities come to where the people are and not for the people searching for them. Hospitals, shopping malls, drugstores or pharmacies, gymnasiums, schools, colleges and universities are within the vicinity. If you get to a mall, you already have everything you need. You don't have to go to another place, everything is in one place.

Spotless Parks

I was amazed when I saw that even parks were sparklingly clean of litter. Dropping paper or others forms of litter is frowned upon. Most of the time trash cans are readily available, wherever you might be. When Amon Dangarebga returned from England with his family to head the Hartzell High School, he brought with him the culture of picking up papers. When he walked from his office to the classrooms, he stopped to pick up paper himself instead of asking a student to it. The effect was that when we all saw him coming, we automatically looked around to be sure that there was no paper littered around. If there was any, we picked that up. The British and the Americans share this culture of cleanliness.

Winter

I had a hard time trying to explain that winter was not merely frost, which my people were used to in Zimbabwe. I tried to tell them that snow falls like cornmeal thrown in the air that then falls to the ground. Still, it was not easy to for them to grasp the concept of snow. Photos were somewhat helpful. Americans make the best of their environment and even make money out of it. There is skiing on snow. Christmas is called white Christmas as a way of forgetting about the cold and adjusting one's thinking that snow brings something good.

Snow made me to come face to face with American generosity. When I was at the Mennonite Biblical Seminary in Elkhart, Indiana, I had no idea about the pending winter and snow. One day the leaders of First United Methodist Church where I attended arranged for me to go out shopping. I was picked up from the seminary, and we went to a shop owned by a member of the church. I was fitted with every type of winter clothing one could imagine. I still have the winter hat they bought for me. I ended being the most well-prepared student for winter—even more than the American students themselves.

"Hi" as a Greeting

When my fellow students met me on campus, they just said "hi." I did not know what to say in return. It took me some time to get it that all I had to say in return was the same hi. From the look of it, Americans find ways and means of shortening everything and doing it quickly. Hi is a shortcut of extended greetings such as, "Good morning, how are you? . . ." and so forth. You save a lot of time by merely saying hi. The short greeting of hi is contrasted with scenes that I have witnessed in Mutare many times, where some elders will move out of the road in order to take time and greet each other in the traditional way of accompanying the greetings with some clapping of hands. I also look forward to a time when we will also shorten the form of greetings with some moderation along the way.

"Have a Nice Day"

The other puzzle was the expression, "Have a nice day!" I did not understand why someone thinks of appreciating a day and its weather. It was later on that I realized that good weather in America is not a given. The weather can turn hostile, and you may be under some weather alerts for your own safety. This was true when we were at Illinois State University. We had to be tuned to weather channels to keep abreast about some weather predictions. So, "have a nice day" was a way of giving some thanks for a having a beautiful day. In Zimbabwe, I grew up with the feeling that good weather was a normal and obvious expectation almost on a daily basis. In fact, I have heard that Zimbabwe is one of the countries in the world with the best weather. I don't have evidence for that.

However, with the rise of cyclones as a result of climate change, we might also be heading into more turbulent weather patterns.

Appointments

In the United States, it seems that for most anything you might want to do that will involve another person, you must make an appointment first. There are few spontaneous occasions of fellowshipping that happen outside appointments. These appointments must be honored as prescribed. If you are going to visit for an hour, you need adjust the fellowship to fit into the agreed-upon minutes. It is common in Africa, or should I say in Zimbabwe, to have someone just pass by your house and come in and end up taking an hour or more, regardless of what you might have been doing. Things are changing in Zimbabwe, but it will likely be misunderstood if people are told that you don't have time to see them. That is regarded as rude, and you will soon be the bad guy in the neighborhood. When you understand the fact that American life is one of schedules, then you appreciate the setting up of these appointments.

Sleep In

I cannot hide that I enjoyed the culture of sleeping in. Actually, sleeping in means more than just sleeping; it means that one is independent as an individual to do what he or she pleases. Sleep is also related to the issue of appointments, which we have discussed. In order to sleep in without disturbance, you must be assured that no person will just come without warning. American life is a life of individualism without obligations. Yes, there are responsibilities, but they have limits and the limits should not be taken for granted. In my culture, you will hear the voice of someone coming: "Are you still asleep in here? This is the time to get out of bed!" In the true sense of communal life, people feel that they are free to give instructions to the other at will. No one really takes offense. The problem is usually only noticed by those of us who have been exposed to other lifestyles.

Lock Your Door

It is matter of high security in America that you lock your house door at all times. When I returned to Zimbabwe, I began locking my office. My brother, who was also teaching at the same school, asked me why I locked my office door even when I was inside. I told him that it was a habit that I picked up in America, where it is a must for security reasons that you lock your door. In Zimbabwe, especially in the rural areas, people are not preoccupied with locking the door, even when they are down the road tending a garden. What is there in that hut are the same items you will find in the next hut. Suspicion develops when people begin to live differently from one another. Locking the door in America is not just to protect your property but also your life. There is the gun culture, which is now a matter of concern among the Americans themselves.

Car theft is different in Zimbabwe. Cars are lined along a street, and for the most part, they stay right where they are parked. If there are car thefts, what happens is that the thief takes the car and drives to point B and leaves it there for the owner to find later. Those who take what does not belong to them usually go for money or precious stones, not clothes or household items.

Me First

When I was attending classes at Candler School of Theology, Emory University, I stayed with a couple of elderly people who had been serving in Zimbabwe as missionaries. The wife was a medical doctor and the husband was an art teacher at Old Mutare Mission. While they were at Old Mutare Mission, I was their pastor as well. They influenced Greater and me in matters of self-care. They encouraged us to take a weekend off and go away from the Mission for some time of rest. We did that occasionally and benefited a lot health wise. When they were back in America the husband had retired while the wife continued to work at a hospital in Atlanta. They continued with their habit of taking a weekend off every month. What surprised me was that one of their children and his wife came to visit the parents. They made an error of not knowing the exact weekend the parents were going to be away. They arrived after the parents had already packed the vehicle and were ready to leave. They talked with their children through the windows of the car because they were about to go. The children seemed to understand, and they bade each other goodbye. The parents went off for their weekend away, and the children returned to their state. In my culture we would have adjusted our plans to accommodate the children.

Down to Earth

Americans are generally down-to-earth type of people. They can adapt to situations without much hassle. I had a colleague bishop who had come to be with us in Zimbabwe during the annual conferences. We had some inconveniences where were staying. I thought that she was going to be miserable and complain. That did not happen at all; instead, we joked about what had happened. With other people it might have been a disappointing situation throughout her visit. In dressing Americans are casual and relaxed. Dressing up goes with the occasion, such as Sunday service, a wedding, or a funeral.

Cultural differences are interesting. In my culture, if you dress well at a funeral, it seems to others that you are not mourning the deceased wholeheartedly. This is also changing, but it is still the norm in some parts of the country. When eating, Americans are not always formal in using fork and knife. They can hold their food with bare hands without any second thought. In African culture food is handled by hand in most cases, but this is not about being casual; there may not be a choice, and your hands are the only utensils available.

Owning a Car Is a Necessity

It is common to see students at American colleges and universities driving cars. In some countries, including Zimbabwe, owning a car is still a form of achievement. A teacher might be looking forward to the time he or she will be able to afford to buy a car. In America, a personal car is necessary for transport. In many places you don't see people walking to and from places unless they are walking for exercise. In fact, one of the reasons people in my country yearn to obtain a degree or any other appropriate form of training is to be able to buy a car and to acquire other related items.

Self-Contained Country

Many Americans grow up with a feeling that their country is the only important one in the world. For example, baseball championship games among teams are called the World Series. For some Americans, the world is contained in their country. To complicate matters, especially for children, schools seem not to emphasize the teaching of geography. We hope that this isolationist approach to the world will change.

Once when we were visiting eastern Kansas to cultivate some partnerships, we visited a number of churches. After a service at one of the churches, we came and stood by the door to greet congregants. An older adult woman made a remark as she was shaking hands with me, "Welcome to our little corner of the world." Americans often don't see their country as a little corner of the world, although it is a true observation that the woman made. I knew even before she said it that she had visited a number of other countries in the world. She went on to name the countries she had been to and beyond, and I could then put her expression of the little corner of the world in a meaningful context.

Generous People

I found Americans to be generous people. If you look at generosity nation to nation, that could be seen differently. But here I am concerned with people-to-people relationships. I have already referred to the supply of winter clothes. Add to that the scholarships that saw me through the colleges and universities. Some of the money was raised by the people I was worshipping with. I knew who was paying for university studies.

Conclusion

In the midst of shortcomings here and there, the United States is one of the countries that has done its best in improving the welfare of its people. There are glaring challenges of race relations, which we hope will improve and that the doors of dialogue will remain open among themselves.

5

AFRICA UNIVERSITY WAS MY CRUCIBLE

In their article "Crucibles of Leadership," Warren G. Bennis and Robert J. Thomas describe crucibles like this: "Extraordinary leaders find meaning in—and learn from—the most negative events. Like phoenixes rising from ashes, they emerge from adversity stronger, more confident in themselves and their purpose and more committed to their work. . . ."[1] Such transformative events are called crucibles—a severe test or trial. Crucibles are intense, often traumatic, and always unplanned." Not all crucibles are traumatic. "Others are positive, yet profoundly challenging. Whatever the shape, leaders create a narrative telling how they met the challenge and became better for it."

My crucible at Africa University was positive. What made it a crucible was the awesome experience of establishing a university as one of the pioneer staff. What I got out of that experience has served me well in my ministry as an episcopal leader.

The story of Africa University cannot be separated from the establishment of The United Methodist Church in Zimbabwe. So, a brief background is in order. The establishment of The United Methodist Church in Zimbabwe is linked to the name of Bishop Joseph Crane Hartzell. Upon his election as bishop in 1897, the bishop had some time of reflection. He had a conviction that somewhere in Southern Africa under the Anglo-Saxon spread of civilization, Methodism should have a foothold.

The Dream

"Dream" is a key word embedded in the story of Africa University. The university is a product of a dream. Dr. Angella Current-Felder even wrote a book on Africa University with the title *The School of Dreams in the Valley of Hope*. Dr. Patrick Matsikenyiri, one of the renowned choir directors at Africa University, composed a song called "The Dream." The song has earned itself the place of being the anthem of the university. The story of this dream goes back to Bishop Hartzell, who in his prayerful moments on Chiremba Mountain heard voices of people converging in the valley. With the establishment of Africa University, the dream was fulfilled.

Enter the General Conference

Two African bishops, Bishop F. Arthur Kulah and Bishop Emilio de Carvalho, got some inspiration beyond anyone's imagination. They observed with a critical eye that The United Methodist Church had established high schools throughout Africa, but the denomination had not yet thought of establishing a university for Africa. This clarion call for higher education through the effort of the church got the attention of many. The Board of Higher Education and Ministry picked up the challenge and formulated a petition to be presented at the General Conference in 1988, calling for the establishment of Africa University

The General Conference passed the petition to establish a university in Africa. Then the process for selecting the site started in earnest. A site selection committee was put in place. There were some basic requirements in selecting where in Africa the university would be established. The United Methodist Church would have to be well established in that country of choice. English should be the official language. The country should be peaceful with a promising future. Further, there had to be land for the university.

Site Selection Committee

In his deliberations with Bishop Hartzell on the land for the church at Old Mutare Mission that the bishop was inquiring about, Cecil John Rhodes described how beautiful the Eastern Highlands of Zimbabwe were. Although Rhodes had his imperialist objectives, his description of the eastern region of Zimbabwe as one of the most beautiful areas of the country cannot be disputed even in the present day. He went on to describe a section of the country known as Nyanga, calling it New England.

To meet the requirement for land for the university, Bishop Abel Temdekayi Muzorewa led the Zimbabwe Annual Conference to cede the area of the Old Mutare Mission farm to be given to the university. That foresight and quick action was an important leverage for presenting the case for Zimbabwe as the future home for the university to the site selection committee. At the time when the committee visited Old Mutare Mission, I was the pastor-in-charge and the station chairman. We organized the way and approach of engaging with the committee, following the mandate that Bishop Muzorewa had given us. Rev. Dr. Morgan Johnson, a missionary who taught art at the Hartzell

High School, did a marvelous job of painting some sceneries of the Eastern Highlands. We maximized the description of beauty that Rhodes had already noted.

Pastor-in-Charge

I need to take a step back in this story of Africa University as a crucible in my life. As I planned to return home from my studies in the United States, I expressed my wish during consultation to be appointed somewhere in Harare. I had some plans to do some research at the National Archives of Zimbabwe in Harare. Rev. Elliot Jijita, who was the administrative assistant to the bishop, responded in a telegram, "Appointment: Harare No, Old Mutare Yes." I am not quoting the exact words of the telegram, but the gist of the message is well captured here.

When I graduated from Epworth Theological College, my first appointment was at Old Mutare Mission. Now as I was finishing my studies overseas, again my appointment was at Old Mutare Mission. I was so disappointed, and I had the feeling that things were not working well for me. Nevertheless, I accepted the appointment to be the assistant pastor to Rev. Elias Nhamoinesu Mumbiro, who was the pastor-in-charge. I was also the appointed teacher at the high school in African History for Form 5 and 6 (comparable to junior college) and school's chaplain.

It is interesting that from 1971 to 1974, Reverend Mumbiro and I were the only two students for The United Methodist Church who were graduating in 1974. Now, from mid-1984 to 1986, we worked together at Old Mutare Mission. Reverend Mumbiro had also just returned from studies in the United States a bit earlier than I had. In 1987 he was appointed the district superintendent of the Mutasa Makoni District. I then became the pastor-in-charge from 1987 to 1991. I was so fortunate to be the pastor-in-charge at Old Mutare Mission. Old Mutare Mission became the hub of all the activities that had to do with the establishment of Africa University. Visits from boards and commissions were received at Old Mutare Mission. The demands of high-quality leadership with no excuses were highlighted. We learned on the job about how to deal with high-powered delegations, which included church leaders from different countries throughout the world. I thank God that we lived up to the demands of the moment.

Nyadire Mission First Choice

It is important to take note that before Bishop Muzorewa led the conference to offer land at Old Mutare Mission, his first choice was for the Africa University to be built at Nyadire Mission. Unfortunately, when the bishop led his delegation to Nyadire to meet with the leaders at the mission, the community was not yet ready to have that proposed university. The result was that the visit by the bishop and his entourage was aborted because of protests. Everything is now water under the bridge.

Local Committee

When it became clear that the site selection committee was commissioned and ready to start its work by visiting the prospective sites in Africa, we at Old Mutare Mission established a local committee. No one had told us about how to prepare for such a make-or-break presentation to such a high-powered delegation.

As we met with the station executive to map out our preparation and strategy in planning, the executive came up with the idea of a local committee. The local committee was mandated to prepare a portfolio to be presented before the site selection committee. At the end of the presentation, the write-up was to be presented to the chair of the commission. Members of the local committee came from the existing departments at the Old Mutare Mission. These were the church, hospital, school, and the mission farm.

I have already made reference to Dr. Johnson, who was an art teacher at the high school. He made glamorous sketches of the Eastern Highlands. We included the government plans of developing the Beira Corridor entering into Mutare, the nearby town to Africa University. In addition, there was talk of the proposed airport north of the present location of Africa University. This proposed development of the airport was to open new possibilities in transportation related to the university. International students would have fast access to the university by air instead of driving by road from Harare to Mutare. Such infrastructure of the Beira Corridor and the airport meant development for the good of the university in the near future.

My role as the pastor-in-charge and the station chairman was to brief District Superintendent Reverend Mumbiro about the preparations and the progress that we were making. He in turn informed the bishop. Everyone was in the loop of communication. We got help from suggestions coming from the bishop's office.

Hospitality Committee

In Shona culture there is a saying that says: "*Ukama Igasva Huno Dzadziswa Nekudya*"—Relationships are not complete, they can only be fulfilled by eating together. Africans top off their events by eating a meal together. We decided to put in place a hospitality committee. The key members were Mrs. Mukono, the wife of the deputy head at the high school, and Mrs. Maenzanise, the high school domestic science teacher. Other members came randomly from the other departments. There was no budget for hosting these visitors for the purpose of planning for the university. We levied the departments at the mission. There was a spirit of oneness, which made it possible for us to raise adequate funds for hosting the would-be guests from the search committee and any other visitors after them.

We did not have a hall nearby to host the visitors for lunch. Meals were prepared at the parsonage. We used the good shade from the trees at the parsonage. We were well equipped as far as utensils were concerned. As part of her preparations for her household, my wife, Greater, had purchased a variety of utensils and shipped them to Zimbabwe. These, in addition to what the mission had, served our purpose well.

When the site selection committee came to Zimbabwe, the bishop's office told us the day and time of their visit at Old Mutare Mission. On the day of the visit, everything went on as planned. The committee then went on to the actual site for the proposed university. It was still mostly trees and tall grass, with the harvested cornstalks here and there in the fields.

Announcement of Choice

For announcing its decision about where to build Africa University, the site selection committee decided to meet in the evening at the Wise Owl Hotel in Mutare. They deliberated on what they had seen in different localities. The chair of the committee announced the decision that Africa University was to be built at Old Mutare Mission on the land the annual conference had donated already. This was a momentous decision that ushered in an avalanche of activities now geared to the actual establishment of the university.

When I say Africa University is my crucible for leadership, it is because of the unprecedented opportunities that all of a sudden opened up for me. Because of my position as the pastor-in-charge and the station chairman at the mission, the chair of the site selection committee decided that I should be present at their gatherings as an observer. My being present became the norm for all the subsequent meetings of different committees that had anything to do with the establishment of the university. I was then privileged to be among the leaders of The United Methodist Church at the highest level internationally. I was exposed to the ways and means of exercising leadership with expertise. In the site selection committee, there were experienced and skilled leaders in the area of Higher Education and Ministry, such as Dr. Roger Ireson, Dr. James Laney, and others of similar caliber. Not many people have had the opportunity of witnessing the establishment of an emerging university of both a continental and global nature.

A Leap of Hope

Even before the granting of the charter, the new university began to recruit staff, starting with the vice chancellor, deans of faculties, and the pioneer faculty staff. I am one of those who applied to be a staff member in the Faculty of Theology. The first vice chancellor, Professor John Wesley Zwomunondiita Kurewa, and the dean of the Faculty of Theology, Bishop David Kekumba Yemba, were already in place.

My interview took place in London, the United Kingdom of Great Britain, where other meetings of the university were taking place. In 1991 Professor Kurewa and I boarded the plane together for a flight to the United Kingdom. My time for the interview came. I answered the questions to the best of my knowledge. I was immediately told of the outcome. I was successful to join the Faculty of Theology in the Department of Pastoral Theology. After the interview, I just waited for my day to return home. I left Professor Kurewa and the team deliberating on the other affairs of the university.

The Charter

The process entered an anxious time of negotiating for the granting of the charter by the government of Zimbabwe. There were private universities by the churches in Zimbabwe operating without a charter. This means that those universities were not accredited and therefore not authorized to offer degrees. The United Methodist Church had made the granting of the charter its prerequisite for the university's existence. In the meantime, the government of Zimbabwe established a Council of Higher Education to look into the establishment of private universities in Zimbabwe. The council came to Old Mutare Mission for its meeting with The United Methodist Church leaders. Bishop F. Herbert Skeete and others flew from the United States for that meeting. Bishop Skeete led the church in the deliberations with the government council. I was there, seated in my privileged corner, absorbing all I could about what leadership means at different levels of the church. It was a joy observing Bishop Skeete navigating the complex questions and nuances that the council members were raising. He led with the acumen expected of a bishop of The United Methodist Church. Bishop Skeete delved into the abilities of The United Methodist Church in running universities as testified by the many institutions under its jurisdiction or related to the church. One can say he rose and met the demands for leadership in the moment.

One of the members of the council whom I remember was a United Methodist church pastor, Rev. Dr. Micah Chinoda, who was at the time working in the government. He had earned a PhD in Education in Nashville, Tennessee, in the United States. We had known each other because we had worked together as pastors in the church. After some deliberations, the council requested for some time alone. All of us including Bishop Skeete vacated the room. The meeting took place in the Hartzell High School staff room. I always wonder how Reverend Chinoda contributed to the deliberations in the council. One thing was clear, he had demonstrated his abilities as a leader, so much so that the government of Zimbabwe had entrusted him and others with this pioneering responsibility of granting charters to private universities.

A Journey of Faith

Other processes took place in different arms of the government including the parliament. At the end of 1991 I left Old Mutare Mission and started employment with Africa University, which still was in the process of being established. Starting in January 1992, I was employed by Africa University as a lecturer, where there was no university yet. There was a hive of activities to prepare course descriptions in the university. I remember very well the few teaching staff huddled in a room at the Green Glades apartments in Mutare. Each had a corner and desk for work. It is so satisfying that when I hold the Africa University prospectus and note the contribution I made in making course descriptions in the Department of Pastoral Theology.

Each day created its own routine. There was no fixed schedule yet. Groundbreaking was set to take place for the administrative block. For the preparation I was assigned to negotiate with a White farmer, Mr. Barry, for the supply of water with a tanker. That was the time I discovered that even farmers have offices. Mr. Barry's office was in the middle of the fields. When I got in his office, I noticed that dates were marked by what crop should be either planted or harvested. He agreed to supply all the water the university needed for the groundbreaking ceremony.

The minister of higher education, Mr. Karimanzira, came to do the groundbreaking. That event ignited some hope and enthusiasm among the staff and well-wishers. The charter was finally granted, and the university opened to the students in March 1992.

Preparations for the Opening of the University

During the waiting period for the charter, long-term preparations for the opening of the university to students were taking place. The church had put in place Volunteer in Mission teams to come and make some needed renovations to the old farm buildings. Offices, classrooms, and libraries were created out of those old buildings. Those Volunteers in Mission were dedicated people with a spirit of self-sacrifice that I had not witnessed before.

They raised their own funds to purchase materials, sometimes including the purchase of their own tickets. Each team came with artisans of a variety of skills: building, carpentry, roofing, flooring, and more. Here and there they got some assistance from the university in order for work to move smoothly.

In due course the first faculties of theology and agriculture had a home at the old campus. The university authorities still do a good job of preserving the old campus structures. Every building at the old campus has its own history. The office of the first registrar, Mrs. Constance Mafarachisi, is the small grass-thatched building that greets visitors as they enter the old campus. That old campus is loaded with the story of the journey that Africa University has traveled.

I witnessed visionary leadership in practice. One day I was visiting with a friend, a medical doctor who studied at Oxford University. He told me that their first lecture was what he called "The Medical Tour at Oxford University." I thought to myself, one could take a leadership tour in visionary leadership by taking students through the old campus at Africa University. Refurbishing of the old buildings was no place for people who feel comfortable only in operating in situations where everything was already provided.

Even as we opened the university in March 1992, a number of things were not yet in place. But we forged ahead, while at the same time polishing up what was still remaining. Our students were also in the pioneering mood. They were real trailblazers in making do with what was available. Both staff and students crammed into the mini bus, which ferried them to and from the campus to Mutare. Students lived in rooms at the Glen Glades Apartments, along with some staff who occupied the other rooms.

My Take from Africa University

There were a number of takeaways from my years at Africa University. These lessons were helpful in my episcopal supervision later on.

Taking Risks

Africa University would not have been established if the leadership wanted complete assurance that everything was well supplied and in place. The leaders were ready to take risks. Advertisements for students to apply went out long before the charter was granted. When the students arrived, there was nothing to show them that resembled a university. Orientation was in future tense: "The library shall be built here and there will be a classroom block there." At a time when anyone would have been excused for raising doubts, that was the very time when the leaders were so convincing and hopeful beyond any doubt.

When I was a bishop, the time came for us in the Zimbabwe Episcopal Area to build two head offices, one in each conference, and we did not hesitate. The money needed for each building was in the millions. We encouraged each other and managed to build those two big buildings. Risk-taking and exuberant hope were the bedrock of success. It was at Africa University that I galvanized this spirit of confidence in preparing to do the extraordinary with ordinary people in the church pews on Sundays.

Fast Pace and Adaptation

The Book of Discipline of The United Methodist Church has a section where it refers to the type of leadership needed in the church. It should be a leadership style that understands mode and pace. In leadership one has to be agile. Do whatever you might do fast. Fast pace marked the way work was done at Africa University. There was no room for a sluggish way of doing things. In the church we used to do groundbreaking or dedications one per Sunday. How many Sundays were there to be able to do groundbreakings and the dedications throughout the episcopal area? There were not enough Sundays for such voluminous work.

When I became a bishop of the church, I took a leaf from Africa University, where we did some groundbreakings after the chapel service on Wednesdays, when the board of directors was in session. Groundbreakings and dedication of the other church buildings apart from churches were done during the week. Only the dedication of sanctuaries was done on Sundays. With such adaptation, much of the backlog for the groundbreaking and dedications was completed in due course. Three or more groundbreakings were done on one day. Both fast pace and adaptations were combined to produce phenomenal results.

Time Management

Anyone who has taught a class where you share both time and space is aware of how critical it is for the smooth running of a university. Of course, time management is something I learned early in my life. During my education, especially at higher levels of training, I had to manage time carefully. But at Africa University, there was an additional component. There was so much work in the early years of the university. Each staff member served on almost every committee. There were still few staff to be able to allocate one or the other to selected committees. You might be a member of the senate, at the same time as you were serving on the Scholarship Committee (which reports to the senate), or a member of the Student Affairs Committee. Before you knew it, you were reporting to yourself.

There was so much work that the end of classroom work meant that we were all headed into administrative work in the evenings. In the early years of the university, it was the norm to leave the campus for Mutare at ten o'clock in the evening and even later. I am an early riser. Earlier in this book I have made mention of how my elder sister used to wake me up to work the fields before I went to school. That practice of doing work early became etched in my work ethic. Even to this day when there is so much to do, I work best from three o'clock to six o'clock in the morning. That routine enabled me to absorb the unrelenting pressure of work we had to go through in establishing Africa University.

I carried on with these practices in doing my work of supervising the church. I tease my district superintendents that I would be fine with doing groundbreakings or dedications at four o'clock in the morning. My background of studying by correspondence while at the same time working meant balancing my time well. While studying at universities, I finished my research assignments for seminars at an average of two weeks before the due date. Of course, I was careful not to hand in the papers to professors early because they might think I was not giving enough time to my assignments. So, I handed in my papers not too early and not too late, either. That worked well for me, since I got As on papers that I researched and wrote two to three weeks before the due date. To this day, I don't want to procrastinate in doing what must be done.

While I agree with the general observation that the work of the bishop in The United Methodist Church is demanding, I am still of the opinion that it is doable. The background that made me who I am in the field of work has prepared me reasonably well for the office of the bishop with its demands in the African context.

Continuous Learning

The Africa University Board of Directors brings together leaders from around the world. They bring a variety of skills and styles of doing work, which provide a vibrant platform for learning. Terms in leadership and cutting-edge knowledge flow freely in conversations of the board. People who make up the board have a long history of working with expertise in various careers. I can very well say that I find the Africa University Board of Directors a hub of continuous learning.

Long-Term Planning

Long-term planning is at the center of the way the university keeps an eye focused on the future, using clear benchmarks to track progress: there is always the when, how, and where in measuring that progress. For Africa University, figures play an important role: nothing is covered in generalizations. Numbers of students, staff, and different classifications are the way of doing business at Africa University. Africa University is a believer and practitioner in the saying "What can be counted can be measured."

Disaster Response Office

I was given the responsibility to establish a Disaster Response Office at Africa University, for which I needed a variety of skills. I had to go to Nashville, Tennessee, in the United States, for some days of training and orientation in preparation for setting up that office. At Africa University, if you got additional work, that did not mean that any other responsibilities in your portfolio were transferred to others. I was still responsible for all my other duties in the Faculty of Theology. I worked in conjunction with an office in Geneva called ACT. Hiring a secretary and the establishment of the office, including the furnishing process, was done in a matter of days. Literature to describe what the office and the program stood for was in place as a matter of urgency.

What I have learned in leadership is that whatever one does must be done well. That very experience will one day later serve you well. My experience in writing course descriptions for the Department of Pastoral Theology prepared me for when I faced the task of producing the literature for the new office and its program. Everything was needed "yesterday." The slogan was, Action Now! In order to accomplish our work, we were literally on the run. I look at all these developments as my crucible while I was at Africa University.

Wrestling in the Valley of Dreams

The way the first vice chancellor, Professor Kurewa, pursued Professor Mphuru to be the dean of the Faculty of Agriculture turned into an epic story for Africa University. Under pressure to have the dean of the Faculty of Agriculture in place in due course, Professor Kurewa flew to Tanzania in search of Professor Mphuru, who had already applied for the post but was no longer showing strong interest to take up the job. When Professor Kurewa arrived at the University of Dar Es Salaam, where he thought Professor Mphuru was, he was told that he was not there and had gone out of town to some rural area far away.

Professor Kurewa was not going to give up. He took up a journey of tracking Professor Mphuru into the villages of Tanzania. By the time he got where Professor Mphuru had gone to, it was dark. Professor Kurewa fell into a pit and dislocated his ankle. The good news was that he was able to find professor Mphuru, and the agreement for the professor to be dean of the Faculty of Agriculture was sealed.

But Professor Kurewa's ankle had dislocated and was hurting. Back home, the vice chancellor was limping for some weeks. At Africa University we turn everything, even that which brings pain, into a source of hope. The story developed that Professor Kurewa wrestled with the messenger of God in the Valley of Dreams in search of Professor Mphuru. The search for Professor Mphuru became an epic story of determination for Africa University.

The Academy and the Traditional Culture

Africa University blends the academic world with the traditional culture in the surrounding area. The university is situated in the area of Chief Mutasa. There is a tradition which has developed where Chief Mutasa is brought from his residence to attend selected events at the university. Everything else comes to a standstill so that the gathering of students, staff, and guests take time "*kuwombera mambo*," that is, to express honor and greetings to the chief. A person who is familiar with the traditional way of greeting the chief is requested to be present and lead the congregation in expressing greetings to the chief. Sometimes the role is taken up by one within the entourage of the chief. Africa University is so unique in many ways, especially in this case.

Action

Dr. James Salley, associate vice chancellor for Institutional Advancement for Africa University and longtime chief fundraiser, is an action-oriented person. We developed a catch word to remind and motivate ourselves that we were at Africa University for action—nothing more, nothing less. To this day when I meet with Dr. Salley, the greetings are embedded in the word *action*. When we say that to each other, everything else follows. My everything in leadership is summarized in the word *Action*. You can talk as much as you want, but if there is no action, nothing will come of it. In other words, leadership is about implementation. Translate words, theories, and strategies into doing, and then you will accomplish. Nothing can replace action in leadership. I was deeply influenced by the atmosphere of action that Dr. Salley exuded as we undertook our work at Africa University. Even as I supervise the church, it is about action and more action.

The Language of Africa University

Let me close this chapter by describing what I call the language of Africa University. I have come to learn and understand that it is important to grasp the terms and names in a particular organization. Without a clear grasp of the terms that constitute the culture of an institution, one's ability to lead effectively can be hampered. Africa University is the crucible that afforded me the opportunity to learn and absorb the terms in The United Methodist Church; this understanding enlightened me and my work as a bishop of the church. In The United Methodist Church, new terms or concepts come up at a rapid rate. Recently we have been plunged into the language of disaffiliation. Failure to grasp such terms with all the embedded implications might mean distorted leadership in the church.

Bishop Joseph Crane Hartzell

If you are connected with Africa University, you know who Bishop Hartzell was. The establishment of The United Methodist Church in Zimbabwe is closely linked to Bishop Hartzell. It was Bishop Hartzell who had a vision as he went up the Chiremba Mountain to pray. On the mountain he heard many voices of people converging in the valley. Hence the "Dream" as a key word for Africa University.

Bishops Kulah and De Carvalho

These two bishops had inspiration that led to the idea that a university should be established by The United Methodist Church in Africa.

Apportionments

Let me take this opportunity to take a step beyond what this book is meant for and to thank the United Methodist bishops and their people for supporting Africa University through their conferences in raising apportionments. Apportionments are not for Africa University only, but if there is an institution in The United Methodist Church where apportionment is talked about with appreciation, it is at Africa University.

Chiremba Mountain

This is the mountain near Old Mutare Mission where Bishop Hartzell climbed for prayer. Again, through his creativity, Dr. Salley has made reference to the Chiremba Mountain in numerous and humorous but effective ways for Africa University. You can wear a Chiremba Mountain pin as a donor to Africa University, and to wear that pin is to attain high recognition within the Africa University community.

Acacia Tree

The acacia tree is found all over the campus at the university and in the surrounding areas. It is that tree on the logo of the university: "Investing in Africa's Future."

Conclusion

Africa University gave me an exposure to the world of leadership that I would not trade for anything. It was a time for work wrapped in hope. The conditions did not allow any other way of working but to forge teamwork. I shall forever cherish the opportunity and privilege I had to be part and parcel of Africa University.

6

WE HAVE AN ELECTION

Background

Elections to the episcopacy have a long tradition in The United Methodist Church. It is interesting to note that the founding father of Methodism, John Wesley, was averse to the whole idea of having bishops. He just did not want his movement to have bishops for its leaders. Episcopacy is a development that took place against his wishes. Along the way, he referred to himself as one practicing "scriptural episcopacy," whatever he meant by that. It is not clear why Wesley did not want bishops to lead the church.

If he was concerned that bishops represented too much power, then he did not manage to stop people from seeing him as one who was too powerful himself. Along the way, Wesley was seen as an authoritarian. At one point he was labeled as "Pope John." His response to some who became critical of him in terms of abuse of power was to point them to the door to leave if they so desired. Either way The United Methodist Church as we know it took the path for bishops in the church.

In the earlier years of the denomination, election of bishops took place at the General Conference. Now, bishops are elected by the lay and clergy delegates in each regional area (jurisdictional and central conferences) every four years following regular sessions of the General Conference.

Given where we are now regarding the election of bishops, it is difficult to assess which approach is better than the other. What led to the change from electing bishops at General Conference to the way things are now? Did the denomination really move away from having bishops elected at the General Conference? My response is, not really. The General Conference still has considerable influence regarding who will be elected a bishop, even though it is in a remote manner.

There is an established tradition that the one who is elected first becomes the head of the delegation to the General Conference and stands a good chance of being considered a viable candidate to the episcopacy. In other words, the annual conferences, central conferences, and the jurisdictions are still under the spell of the influence of the General Conference as far as the election of bishops is concerned.

Africa election of bishops is a closed process, shrouded in secrecy. I was surprised by the openness of the women bishops in The United Methodist Church who narrated their experiences of their elections as bishops in their book, *Women Bishops of the United Methodist Church: Extraordinary Gifts of the Spirit*. After reading the book and one or more other sources on episcopal elections, I felt the urge to reflect on my own election. It took some effort to weave a narrative of how it all happened, because in hindsight, the process for my election to the episcopacy took a long and winding way. The long process took place without the obvious indicators that it was an intentional process leading to my being elected bishop of the church.

Tradition of the Conference Secretary

In Zimbabwe there is an established tradition that for one to be elected the bishop of the church, that person would have served as the conference secretary. Bishop Muzorewa, Bishop Christopher Jokomo, and I have served as conference secretaries. It is not clear why the position of the conference secretary rose to such prominence regarding being considered a possible candidate for the episcopacy. My assumptions are as follows:

First, the conference secretary works closely with the bishop when the conference is in session. That means that the conference secretary is well positioned to have inside knowledge about how the bishop presides over the annual conference. Second, the conference secretary, by virtue of that position, is thrust into the limelight before the people at the sessions of the annual conference. People are comfortable to have leaders whom they are familiar with. They are hesitant to have leaders who suddenly come before them out of nowhere. In other words, the election of a conference secretary is a way of putting that person on display before the people for them to scrutinize him or her. Third, the conference secretary is expected to attend most of the boards, councils, and committees of the annual conference. In doing so the conference secretary becomes knowledgeable about the work of these entities in the church. The conference secretary knows the church, thus goes the assumption. Fourth, there is the production of the journal of the annual conference. The process of the journal of the conference is viewed as a window by which leaders can assess how efficient the conference secretary is. The earlier the journal gets into the hands of the delegates to the annual conference, the better will be the evaluation the secretary gets as a potential candidate for the episcopacy.

The Zimbabwe Episcopal Area continues to follow this critical assessment in looking for probable candidates for the episcopacy. The good thing is that this is not the only criterion for one to be considered a viable candidate. There are a lot of other areas of ministry and qualifications and skills that are also highly regarded for the possible candidates to possess. The fact still remains though that, whatever the origin of this tradition of seeing the conference secretary as a natural candidate for the episcopacy, this practice has indeed taken root in Zimbabwe.

I understand this tradition as a desperate attempt to try to give some rationale about who should be considered for election to the episcopacy. It is also a clarion call for the church that a deliberate well-thought-out list of expectations for the candidates to meet before they are considered possible candidates for that high office should be put in place. If in the secular world advertisements of different positions put the qualifications needed up front for the would-be applicants, why shouldn't the church do the same?

I am relieved to say that at its meeting in 2016 in Luanda, Angola, the Africa Central Conference engaged in some serious deliberations on the need to make reforms about the process of conducting episcopal elections in the central conference. A number of new expectations were put in place. For one, there will be need for the candidates to provide their CVs (curriculum vitae) to the delegates ahead of time. There will be a write-up about why they think they should be elected to the episcopacy. There will be an interview at the venue of the conference before the delegates. In other words, the central conference removed the determination about who might be elected to the episcopacy from the home front aspirations and put the process into the hands of the delegates. Still there is no sure way of knowing that such a process will produce neat elections to the episcopacy; but one could say it is better than nothing.

Beyond What the Eye Can See

I have already noted that, in my experience, the process of electing a bishop is a long one. The electoral process is not always clearly marked with specific activities and behaviors. As I look back, I now realize that the process that led to my election as the bishop of the church had some people who were nurturing it without me being aware of what was happening behind the scenes. Most people don't usually notice much of what is happening. It is a given that there has to be people of influence interested in a particular individual to be the candidate.

The first Zimbabwe Annual Conference following the 1992 General Conference was held at Mutambara Mission of The United Methodist Church. In The United Methodist Church polity, it is at that annual conference where the new conference leaders are elected for the next quadrennium. When I got to the site of the annual conference, a layperson of considerable influence in the church approached me discreetly. He told me that when my name was raised from the floor for the position of the conference secretary, I should not refuse. I just nodded in agreement, and he went away. I could not figure out what the whole idea was about. It was the first year for our newly elected Bishop Jokomo to lead the church. Why should the position of the conference secretary be an issue at such a time? That was the type of musing my naive mind followed.

When the time came for the nomination committee to present its report, the name of Rev. Shirley DeWolf was on the nomination slate for the position of the conference secretary. When more names were called for, my name was raised from the floor. A second hand was up when the delegate was given the floor, a proposal to close nominations. The motion was supported, and the nominations were closed. When the bishop called for delegates to receive ballots to vote between Reverend DeWolf and me, I won that vote with overwhelming majority. I was the conference secretary and took my position by the side of the bishop. Reverend DeWolf became the vice conference secretary. Although I was not yet clear about the intention, I did understand that politicking was going on. There were already two strong groups mapping out the possible successor to Bishop Jokomo, whenever that opening happened. The group that had nominated Reverend DeWolf was using the decoy approach to cover up their real focus. It would have become too obvious had they elected for the conference secretary the actual candidate they had in mind to succeed the bishop upon his retirement. The tactical approach was to propose the name of Reverend DeWolf, who did not harbor any ambitions for contending for the post of the bishop.

But the group that raised my name did not fall for that ruse. Unfortunately for the other group, they underestimated the possibility of the existence of an undertow to their moves in the conference. We will pick up that thread later.

The Dangarembga Commission

The 1992 Annual Conference pushed for the need to have two annual conferences in Zimbabwe. In response to that expression, Bishop Jokomo set up a commission under the leadership of a renowned layperson in the church in Zimbabwe. Mr. Dangarembga was assigned the task of chairing the commission. He was one of the early Africans to attain a master's degree; studying in the United Kingdom in the 1960s. Upon his return to Zimbabwe, he was appointed as the headmaster of the Hartzell High School.

The commission met for its deliberation in the hall at St. Paul United Methodist Church. As the conference secretary, I was selected to become a member of that commission. The commission proposed the necessary boundaries for the new annual conferences. The two proposed conferences were the Zimbabwe East Annual Conference and the Zimbabwe West Annual Conference. The report of the commission was presented to the annual conference and was adopted. This petition of the Zimbabwe Episcopal Area went to the Africa Central Conference in 2000.

Back to Our Two Groups

Let us return to the election that took place in 1992 at the Mutambara Mission where I was elected the conference secretary. The two groups were aware of the possibility that the annual conference was headed for a proposal for it to be divided into two. What accelerated the process was the erroneous idea that the two annual conferences would mean the creation of two episcopal areas, hence, two bishops. Our people did not yet understand that you can have more than one conference but still have one bishop and thus one episcopal area. It is interesting to note though that the election of a bishop takes some foresight and the necessary subsequent strategic actions, irrespective of whether the candidate is aware of this or not. A strong supportive and knowledgeable team is necessary.

The 2000 Africa Central Conference

The 2000 Africa Central Conference met in Maputo, Mozambique. The Zimbabwe Episcopal Area presented a petition to become two annual conferences. The petition passed that Zimbabwe could then have two annual conferences under one bishop. The people learned then that in order to have two additional bishops, it was the General Conference that had to make that decision. At that central conference, elections were to take place for the leaders for the following quadrennium. I was approached by a woman delegate to the central conference from Zimbabwe. She told me that if my name came up for the position of the general secretary for the Africa Central Conference, I should not turn it down. She went on to emphasize that even though I was already the conference secretary back home, it was still important that I become the general secretary for the central conference. As usual, I gave a nod that I had acknowledged the message. Indeed, my name came up for the position of the general secretary for the Africa Central Conference. I was elected to the position. Without my being aware of it, a lot of canvassing for my name was going on among the delegates. It is even possible that contacts with the other delegates from the other countries might have started long before we even got to Maputo.

Dadaya Annual Conference

Let me backtrack and fill in a few pieces of information from the time when Bishop Muzorewa was still an active bishop. When the Zimbabwe Annual Conference was held at the Dadaya Mission in Masvingo, there was talk that sooner rather than later, the Zimbabwe Area was going to hold nominations for a new bishop to succeed Bishop Muzorewa. One morning soon after the devotion, delegates were in some frenzy, ululating and dancing, supposedly under the spell of some phenomenal power of the Holy Spirit. Rev. Conrad Chigumira, a highly respected clergyperson came to where I was seated and held my hand. He pulled me from my seat, calling from the top of his voice, "*Nhiwatiwa Tungamira Vanhu*," which translated from the Shona language means, "Nhiwatiwa, Lead the People." As he held my hand he headed to the door and I followed not knowing where we were going. A considerable number of people followed and we ended up in a classroom. There were prayers and testimonies. The conference session was delayed until the situation calmed down. We later on returned to the venue and the conference business resumed.

Whatever Reverend Chigumira had in mind when he held my hand, heading out of the conference venue, it was hard to tell. One thing was clear though, many delegates noticed the event with some sense of curiosity. I was at the center of the drama and was a bit taken aback without figuring out what was actually happening. We were dealing with figurative language, which is elusive to the naked eye. Reverend Chigumira had since passed on by the time I became bishop of the church. May his soul rest in peace.

Prayers From Rev. Josiah Chidzikwe

Another elderly retired and well-respected pastor in the Zimbabwe Annual Conference was Rev. Josiah Chidzikwe. When I was the pastor-in-charge at Old Mutare Mission, Reverend Chidzikwe used to pass through the mission on his way to Mutare from Nyakatsapa, his homestead. Each time he passed through, he had a story to tell me about the time he was the pastor-in-charge at the Ehnes Memorial United Methodist Church at Old Mutare Mission. One day I was told that whenever he preached, he saw Jesus Christ standing by his side in the pulpit with him. On another day I was told that he was not going to die because he was going to be raised from the dead. He ended these conversations by holding my hand, leading me to the altar to pray in the Ehnes Memorial Church. He usually prayed for my well-being and for God to brighten my path and fill me with wisdom.

As we were headed for the nominations to elect the successor to Bishop Muzorewa, a pastor told me that Reverend Chidzikwe told him that he, Reverend Chidzikwe, dreamed that I had become bishop. I dismissed such a dream by Reverend Chidzikwe as a figment of his imagination. Everything on the ground was pointing to a different direction in terms of the candidate for election to the office of the bishop. I told the pastor who had told me of Reverend Chidzikwe's dream that Reverend Chidzikwe loved me so much that it was his liking of me that was reflected in his dreams. Reverend Chidzikwe had passed on by the time I became bishop. Again, may his soul rest in peace. We shall come back to dreams later in this chapter.

Enter the 2000 Annual Conference

The 2000 Zimbabwe Annual Conference was held at the Marange Mission of The United Methodist Church. The anticipated report from the Africa Central Conference held in Maputo in 2000 stated that the petition from Zimbabwe for the creation of the two annual conferences was adopted. To prepare for the election of the new leaders for the following quadrennium, the nomination committee met in Harare.

On the eve of the annual conference, Bishop Jokomo called me. He told me in a rather apologetic way that my name was dropped from the list of the nomination committee for me to continue as the conference secretary. My response was to assure the bishop that there was nothing amiss at all. It was good for the church to have a new conference secretary. But knowing what I now know as a bishop, no bishop makes such a call out of the blue. My hunch is that the bishop was not comfortable with the politicking that he detected unfolding before him. What he was attempting to do was to extricate himself from all that was going on. Hence this call and conversation with me. Of course, I might be wrong in making this conclusion.

When the annual conference opened at the Marange Mission, the delegates pushed for the annual conference to be divided as a matter of urgency. They were not in the mood to entertain any further delay.

Instead, the nomination committee went ahead to present its report to the annual conference, including a list of leaders for only one Zimbabwe annual conference. The delegates rejected the report of the nomination committee, which, first, had met away from the venue of the annual conference and second, had not reflected the need for the leaders for the two annual conferences. The debate went on until lunch.

When the session started, my wife, Greater, and I took our time getting back, stopping to admire the flowers at the Marange High School. I was no longer the conference secretary, so there was no hurry in going back to the session of the conference, so I thought. As we were dallying, we saw a woman delegate running in our direction. "Rev. Dr. Nhiwatiwa, the bishop is looking for you!" she called out. I rushed back to the venue and as I entered, Bishop Jokomo beckoned for me to come to the front where he was seated. As I took the indicated chair, the bishop announced to the conference that he had not talked to me in any way. What he was asking was for the conference to allow me to be secretary pro tempore. The delegates approved that proposal from the bishop. The bishop turned to me and whispered that the delegates wanted the conference to be divided, then and there. He went on to ask for suggestions about how we could proceed. I suggested that the delegates go out of the venue and group themselves according to the recommended boundaries presented by the Dangarembga Commission. In those groups, I suggested they should nominate from among the delegates people who will form the nomination committee and make a proposed list of leaders to be elected to lead each annual conference. The bishop followed the suggestions. with minor adjustments.

When the delegates came back, they were now coming back as two annual conferences. Each conference presented the nomination report and voted on it. I was elected the conference secretary of the Zimbabwe East Annual Conference. Since the conference

We Have an Election

in seating was still one annual conference, I continued to be the secretary till the end of that conference session.

Sometime in March 2000 or thereabout, Bishop Jokomo fell sick. The whole episcopal area was plunged into dismay. From that time until the 2004 General Conference, the bishop had not yet recovered. We elected the delegates to both the General Conference and to the central conference. I was elected as the head of the delegation for the Zimbabwe East Annual Conference. When we came back from the General Conference, there was talk that the Zimbabwe Episcopal Area might have elections to elect a new bishop to succeed Bishop Jokomo who had still ill. I was lecturing so much at Africa University that some details at the grassroots of the church escaped my attention.

Later on, we heard that Bishop João Somane Machado of Mozambique was coming to Zimbabawe to meet with the leaders. On the day of his arrival, the leaders were called to go to the airport to receive the bishop. Bishop Jokomo asked me to ride in his vehicle with his driver Mr. Mushoperi. As we drove to the airport, the bishop turned to me and said "I don't want Nhiwatiwa to be involved in anything." I blindly thanked the bishop for his advice, although in truth I did not know what he was referring to. The statement was in third person, as if it were addressed to some other person. In any case, we left it at that.

A lot was in the air after the 2004 General Conference in Pittsburgh, Pennsylvania. A student of mine at Africa University in the Faculty of Theology paid me a visit at lunchtime in my office. He said that he was sent by the elders to tell me that they were thinking of raising my name for the episcopal office and that I should not turn it down. I merely expressed my acknowledgement to the message.

Africa Central Conference in Johannesburg, South Africa

Bishop Machado came to Zimbabwe to conduct the nomination at a jointly held session for the two annual conferences.

The 2004 Africa Central Conference took place in Johannesburg, South Africa. Elections took place, and I was elected bishop assigned to the Zimbabwe Episcopal Area. The title of this chapter, "We Have an Election," comes from the traditional announcement, which is usually made by the chair when the ballot results in an election. In my case there was an observation that led to the emphasis on the "we have an election" statement. In the Africa Central Conference, the practice is to have 75 percent of the ballot for one to be declared elected. When one staff member of the General Board of Global Ministries saw that my votes had reached over 60 percent and called out "We have an election!" The chair was surprised that someone else was calling that an election had taken place. In other areas of the church, only 60 percent is required to have an election. I hope that with the new reforms that the Africa Central Conference put in place while in Angola, this will be the new normal. With the declaration by the chair at the 75 percent vote, the long path to my election to the episcopacy came to an end. In 2008 I was reelected to make me bishop for life.

Elections and Dreams

Earlier I said that I was going to share a dream. Just a few days before the Africa Central Conference gathered at Africa University in 2008 for the elections that made me the bishop for life, I had a vivid dream. I dreamed that I was standing with a group of people by the seashore. A boat floated on its own to where we were standing. The people turned to me and asked me to get into the boat. I protested: How could I go alone into that expansive ocean? Their response was that the boat was different because it did not need anyone to row it forward or steer it. I got in, and all the people did was push it forward with their fingertips. The boat roared forward with such speed that nothing could have stood in front of it. To my surprise, there were people whom I could not recognize on the other side of the ocean, welcoming me with cheers. At that point I awoke. From my own interpretation and experience with dreams, I suspected that it could be a good dream in light of the elections ahead of me. In my readings I also found that other bishops who had been elected to the episcopacy also had dreams that they related to their experiences. I am not saying that having dreams is the case for everyone; one could end up having a negative dream, and what could you do about it?

A Word from Other Voices

Episcopal elections in The United Methodist Church are a major process in the life of the denomination. Others take them lightly while some keep some emotional distance so that if they don't get elected, it will not be a disaster in their life. The general feeling in Africa is that, for elections like those in the church for episcopacy, one must not show any interest in them. To be elected, the wisdom goes, one must not show that he or she is interested. Candidates compete with each other to show that they are not interested at all. How many people buy into that no one knows. The word *campaign* should not be mentioned anywhere during the process.

This approach of being disinterested seems to go back to early times. In his autobiography, *A Magnificent Obsession*, Bishop Cannon cited a German Pietist bishop, Albrecht Bengel: "Worldly honor (like one's shadow) flees from us if we pursue it, but pursues us if we run away from it."[1] It used to be said that the episcopal office searches for its occupant and not the other way around. This is the view Africa and many other areas still want to project. It is anyone's conclusion as to how successful the practice is.

A Paradigm Shift

The election to the episcopacy is changing rapidly. Long ago, Bishop Earl Hunt lamented that election of bishops in The United Methodist Church had become too political. "Its principle is more political than Christian, and there are within it the latent dangers of mediocrity and, much worse, tragic error."[2]

In his book *Magnificent Obsession*, Bishop Cannon describes a conversation between the bishop and a prospective candidate for the episcopal position shows that even the bishop was of the opinion that to be elected one has to contribute as well. The candidate told the bishop that if it were the Lord's will that he was to be elected, then he would be elected; if it was not the Lord's will, then the candidate was not going to be elected. Bishop Cannon responded: "I am certain that it will not be the Lord's will for you to be elected."[3] On second attempt the same candidate told the bishop that he was organizing with support teams. He was elected that second time. This is unfortunate because we seem to be hearing that it is time for the candidates to be involved if they are to be elected to the episcopacy. Well, that is the other side of the coin. What is now happening out there is a mixed bag in the race to the episcopacy. There will always be the reminder that it is a God-driven election, and that is true. But there is also the reality that the pretension of candidates acting disinterested is fading away.

A bishop colleague shared her election story, saying that some women clergy from another conference called her to express their support for her to be the candidate for the episcopacy. Her response was "We don't do this in our conferences."[4] The clergy women responded "Well, we do now."[5] The prospective candidate shared with the women clergy that she was not sure whether she was called to the episcopacy. One woman in the group responded, "Perhaps this is a part of your call."[6]

Again, from Bishop Cannon: "The office of the bishop is seldom if ever thrust upon anyone. It generally comes to those who have long sought after it and have used their own talent as well as all the help they could get from friends to attain it."[7] The bishop reflected on his own experience of the election to the episcopacy: "I had been surprised and disappointed over what happened to me in 1964, and I must confess a bit cynical as well, for I came to feel that merit and service and substantial contributions to the General Church count for little in episcopal elections."[8] Elections to the episcopacy depend "almost entirely through the combinations of votes among delegations and political and ingenuity of one or more of their backers in making these combinations."[9]

Conclusion: Personal Perspective

How do I see my election to the episcopacy in light of these views that seem to say the candidate must be ready to do something to improve one's chances of being elected to the episcopacy? I had a solid team of church leaders who were committed to seeing to it that I was elected to the episcopacy. That comes out very clearly in my story. It is also confirmed by the experiences of other bishops. There is need for one to be supported by well-wishers; one cannot elect oneself to the episcopacy. Those supporters should include influential people at the leadership level of the church. In my case therefore I can say that the Lord provided supporters without my even knowing who they were. The role I played was never to put them down by not being clear to them that I was ready and interested to walk with them. Does politicking enter the stage? Yes, indeed. If you are not the one, there will always be those who will not shy away from showing some political dexterity in the process. If it is not your side, then be assured that the other side will move forward.

7

MY EPISCOPACY

Overview

I will open this chapter with a disclaimer that there is no such thing as "My Episcopacy." In The United Methodist Church, episcopacy is carried out in the community of shared polity, ethos, connectional relations, and the conciliar understanding of the Council of Bishops. I, however, have titled the chapter this way because the focus is on what the people and I achieved during my tenure.

In preparing to write this chapter, I did some research on the background of episcopacy.

I found much help in the study that Bishop James Mathews did in his book *Set Apart to Serve*. Bishop Mathews traced the understanding of episcopacy back to John Wesley. In writing to his brother Charles, Wesley stated that he saw himself as "real a Christian bishop as the Archbishop of Canterbury."[1] Wesley was referring to the concept of "scriptural episcopacy." In the Bible, the apostle Paul is viewed as the general overseer of the church. In the eyes of John Wesley, Paul was the "appropriate model" of "scriptural *episkopos*." Bishop Mathews pointed to the text 1 Thessalonians 5:12-13 as a key reference with implications that leaders of the church were labeled as those "who labor among you and are over you in the Lord—"could be taken as the bishops."[2]

What that means is that a case can be made that bishops are referred to in the Bible with some specific texts clearly identifiable. If the text cited from 1 Thessalonians 5:12-13 is referring to bishops then even the people of God are advised on how they view the bishops. Those who accept leadership from the bishops should "esteem them very highly in love because of their work" (1 Thess. 5:13, NRSVUE). Further, Bishop Mathews identified the term *episkopos*, which refers to the function of bishops such as "superintending, overseeing, or visitation."

A chapter that attracted my attention in Bishop Mathews's book is "What Do Bishops Do?" The bishop opened the chapter by noting that people are engaged in the act of "bishop watching"! When people watch bishops, it is to see what the bishops do, compared to what they expect the bishops to do. Every person has an idea of what a bishop should do. This is why there are unfulfilled expectations by the people.

As a starting point of what a United Methodist Church bishop is expected to do, Bishop Mathews reviews the vows bishops make at the time of consecration. What becomes clear is that the episcopacy is not an office of status but of duties and responsibilities.[3] A bird's-eye view of what bishops do, among a variety of tasks reveals these responsibilities: stationing of preachers in their respective charges, presiding officer, pastor of pastors, teaching, administrator, liturgical leader, ecumenical liaison, and spiritual formation.

Bishop William H. Willimon, in his book, *Bishop: The Art of Questioning Authority by an Authority in Question* describes the office of the bishop and its task in contemporary times.[4] He highlights the focus of responsibility for the bishop in areas such as sending pastors, cultivating fruitfulness, leading change, preaching, and leading through the Council. It may be that bishops generally do the same tasks in leading the church, but the difference comes about where they focus attention and the rationale for doing so.

In my episcopacy there was no attempt to reinvent the wheel about how the work of the bishop should be done; the work was to carry on with the task of leading the church in the modest ways possible. The way I carried out my episcopal responsibilities might reflect my own likes and dislikes. Episcopacy is affected by personal interests as much as it also reflects requirements of the office. For me the recurrent question is always, "Am I leading?" I am convinced that a bishop can be anything else as long as the center is held by a clear understanding of leadership. To be a bishop is to be a leader. Even when one exercises the elusive task as showing compassion, the bishop needs to first identify areas in need of empathy. Maybe my focus on leadership reveals my propensity of liking to lead. I do not take leadership lightly, but there is something in me that nudges me in the direction of where leadership is needed.

Convictions

I do not believe that leaders in a given arena may tell people that they do not know what they have accomplished. In the same vein, leaders know which areas were not well done or those that still need some improvements. I am convinced that during my episcopacy in the Zimbabwe Episcopal Area, God gave me dedicated leaders who gave themselves fully to the service of the church. The clergy and the laity were so committed unreservedly to the work of God through The United Methodist Church. We have accomplished a lot of ministry together.

Looking back, I feel that the people whom God gave me to work with deserve a big thank you for being faithful servants of God. Together we have left a mark that will be a reference point for future generations. In the Zimbabwe Episcopal Area, as anywhere else, ours was a collective effort.

Another conviction is that together we ventured into new ways of doing God's work. We expanded new horizons to enrich the ministries of the church. One philosophy that got the attention of almost everyone is the conviction that in whatever we do, we should do it with excellence. We coined a catchy phrase, "claiming higher ground." Everything should be measured by the litmus test of whether it is now better than the way it was before.

This chapter is guided by these and other convictions as we lift up some of the milestones to which my episcopacy could point. Above all, it is all to the glory of God as we brought the people to Christ as disciples meant to transform the world. My approach was to use metaphorical language in giving directions and guidelines to the people about what we were going to be focused on.

Usu Ku Usu

In the Shona language of Zimbabwe, *Usu Ku Usu* means face-to-face. Most of the time when we closed a session of the annual conference, I announced what the focus of the following year would be. During my first quadrennium I informed my cabinet that I was going to put in place a program of visiting in the districts for some days during which I visited each circuit or charge in a particular district. Such arrangements come with changes embedded in them. The district superintendents were used to a system in which they were the ones to invite the bishop as they saw fit. That approach would not have worked for me as one who was fascinated with leadership. There is no way I would have led if all I did was to wait to be invited by the district superintendents. The annual conferences were informed as a way of creating accountability that I was committed to visiting the districts and meeting with the people. I produced a calendar that indicated when I was scheduled to be in a particular district. The calendar was a fait accompli in that there were no negotiations about it unless we encountered some emergency. But in most cases if the emergency affected the district superintendent, then a pastor would have to be assigned to take the bishop around. There was the rationale for coming up with such a program as one of the ways of executing the supervisory work of the bishop. This program was undergirded by specific principles.

Principle 1

When you work with people it is important that you spend some time to meet and get to know them. The people themselves, especially in the African context, yearn to meet their leaders. There were evident expressions of joy when we met in their local settings. They composed or selected appropriate songs to welcome me in their circuits. One such song that became popular during those visits was "Bishop *Mufudzi* Bishop *Mufudzi, Hwai Dzenyu Dzauya Baba!*" that translates as "Bishop is a shepherd, Bishop is a shepherd, your sheep have come, our father!" They usually sang the song either at the time of entering the perimeters of their circuit or at the point of gathering.

Upon my entering into the episcopacy, the people were gracious enough to share through song their way of envisioning the work of the bishop. The bishop is the shepherd, as far as they were concerned. They communicated that perspective clearly through the song. It was a time of listening to hear where they were in their faith journeys in their communities. I took the opportunity to share with and instill in them that it was time for us to work hard and do our own things. I introduced the concept of *chabadza* during those visits. *Chabadza* in Shona means giving a helping hand to one who is already working in the field. I emphasized that the time of expecting churches, parsonages, and other buildings to be built for us with donor funds is over. If we get help it will be coming in the spirit of *chabadza*, that is, helping those who were helping themselves. It was a different message, one that did not encourage donor syndrome. We shall mention *chabadza* again and in detail in the following chapters in this book.

Principle 2

Meeting with people face-to-face is biblical. Time and again the apostle Paul expressed his wish to visit and meet with people through his journeys. His letters reflect a person whose understanding of people was built on the foundation of knowing each other.

Principle 3

Usu Ku Usu is theological in its intent. When we talk about the Incarnation, God coming to live with the people, that was faceto-face at a high theological level. Therefore, *Usu Ku Usu* is incarnational in practice. As a bishop, I found it imperative to bring the episcopal office to the people through the ministry of presence.

Principle 4

Meeting with the people was a form of communication par excellence. Just being with the bishop ignited a lot of thoughts and expectations among the people. Presence is a form of communication. In her article, "Give Yourself Permission to Be Successful," Jeanette Marais has this to say: "Research and my personal experience, have shown that face-to-face interaction is the form of communication that makes people happiest."[5] The platform was set for me to speak to the people and they to me. In addition to the concept of *chabadza*, I told the people that in whatever we did, we should aim higher. When in the rural areas I pointed them to Harare, Bulawayo, or Mutare, to aim for the standards in those cities. I told the rural people that they were the producers of food, so it was in their hands to work and earn a living.

Principle 5

At every level, ministry is relational. Episcopacy cannot be all that different. A bishop is in the business of laying a strong foundation for relationships. Ministry of presence is at the center of my way of doing church. People never get tired of seeing their bishop, at least in the African context. Many times, when I have been in some area, in a shop or wherever, I have been greeted exuberantly: "Nice seeing you so close, Bishop!" Then they take the opportunity of sharing that they yearn to see the bishop more often because they feel encouraged in their lives by just seeing the bishop.

Principle 6

A leader entering a field of work must set a vision with priorities. This face-to-face initiative catapulted me into a position of assessing the needs of the church. Within a short time of meeting with the people, it became clear to me that in each annual conference we had two settings: urban and rural. That meant that each conference had an area that had more resources and the other where resources were scarce. It immediately dawned on me that we needed to gather leaders for a planning session to work out a vision to guide our work in the episcopal area. Without this face-to-face meeting, we would have not gotten there.

Bishop's Mobile College

Another initiative that I put in place in leading the episcopal area was the Bishop's Mobile College. This was a teaching/learning vehicle. The focus of the lessons was on some aspect of the life, teaching, and preaching of John Wesley. The Mobile College touched on areas such as the means of grace as envisioned by John Wesley; money and its use in the eyes of Wesley; Wesley and stewardship; and some other areas. The topics the people seemed to enjoy the most was Money and Stewardship." Wesley's teaching of "Earn all you can, Save all you can, and Give all you can" fascinated the people.

On the topic of stewardship, they usually laughed their lungs out when I mentioned that John Wesley thought that people buy expensive items such as furniture or clothes because they want to show off to their neighbors. They found that teaching resonated with their lives and reflected experiences they were actually going through. The term "mobile college" was so appropriate because the bishop moved around the districts and presented the lessons at a selected venue for the gathering. The lessons were the same throughout the districts.

Maziso Pasi Maziso Mudenga

This term means that everything is up for an assessment after seeing how things were in a given area. There was no area that was left out. The targeted areas were the mission centers, schools, hospitals, and the other units. Instead of telling the people that the bishop was coming to inspect the mission areas, the metaphorical expression caught their attention with some sense of humor. But they still did not miss what the visit meant. A bishop in the African context in The United Methodist Church is likely to have a mission area with schools, orphanages, hospitals or clinics, a farm, or camping grounds to supervise. As I worked on this chapter, I was planning to have a groundbreaking at a camping ground called Mufusire, along the Harare-Mutare Road. There will be the need to encourage the people to raise funds to construct the needed facilities.

During the *Maziso Pasi Maziso Mudenga* initiative, the bishop was the one who selected what to see. It was not a guided tour.

What I have learned is that when the people like what you have taken them through, they will freely give you positive and encouraging feedback. On their own they began to commit themselves to keeping their facilities spruced up at all times. More often than not the heads of institutions appreciated what the *Maziso Pasi* and *Maziso Mudenga* had done for their school. To prepare for the bishop's visit, buildings were repaired and painted. They vowed to keep the practice as an ongoing requirement on their own.

Bishop of Many Names

The work we did during my episcopacy is summarized in the nicknames that I received to reflect the work we did together with my people. In an article by Chenayi Kumuterera, "Bishop Nhiwatiwa Earns Many Nicknames,"[6] these nicknames are catalogued. The names were coined from the names of those programs. The article said, "The names simply reflect the man's practical vision and leadership style." My administrative assistant, Rev. Alan Masimba Gurupira, said, "A person is known by what they do. Bishop Nhiwatiwa is known for introducing practical programs that transform lives, institutions and the church at large. All these names come from the programs he masterminded during his illustrious term of leadership at the helm of the Zimbabwe Episcopal Area."

Usu Ku Usu, which we have already mentioned earlier, comes in as one of my work-related nicknames. The other is the "*Chabadza* Bishop," which we shall say more about. It is interesting though to get some feedback on what the people learned from this article. "The chabadza philosophy gives direction and unique meaning to the episcopal area's international partnerships and local missions. One example is the Zimbabwe-Norway partnership."

"We are truly grateful and appreciate his active participation in the Chabadza concept and in other parts of the partnership between the United Methodist Church in Zimbabwe and

Norway," said Anne Ng Forster, program advisor for the Board of Global Ministries in Norway. "The work done by Chabadza and mission stations like Mutambara, Nyadire and Dendera has a special place in the heart of the Norwegian United Methodist family." The article went on to give details on the Chabadza Zimbabwe Norway Partnership. "It was in 2010 when Bishop Nhiwatiwa and Rev. Tove Odland agreed to carry out a consultative meeting . . . to strengthen the cooperation and partnership." Odland is a deacon at Centralkirken in Oslo. He said, "The spirit of Chabadza can be expanded to include the contribution of dedicated church members who spearhead developmental projects in the church and the community."

Another nickname for the bishop is "Ebenezer Bishop." "During the 2014 Ebenezer Convention, people from the entire episcopal area gathered in the Zimbabwe National Sports Stadium in Harare for celebration and worship. The event emphasized The United Methodist Church's presence in Zimbabwe." "Ranganai Tinashe Dzotizei, Craneborne United Methodist church communicator, recalled the excitement when more than fifty-five thousand congregants turned the stadium "into a sea of blue and red."[7] That blue and red describes the uniform for the women's organization, the Rukwadzano Rwe Wadzimai. "The nation was brought to a standstill as The United Methodist Church hosted the unforgettable, historic Ebenezer Convention initiated by the Ebenezer Bishop."[8]

The BEB Bishop

This acronym BEB pointed to the need for bringing more people to Christ, evangelism, and building infrastructure. It stood for: Bring more people to Christ/Ebenezer Convention/Building New Head offices.

Bishop-in-Residence

The other program was the Bishop-in-Residence. I went into the districts for three days. It was up to the district superintendent and his leaders to decide on the program of action. The people look to those events with anticipation. If I just said that I was coming to visit the district, there would have been little motivation for the people. The use of these uncommon terms energized the people.

Maziso Pasi Maziso Mudenga

Then there is the *Maziso Pasi* and the *Maziso Mudenga* Bishop. The initiative was of seeing and appreciating what the people were doing in their local areas. Add to that the nickname, *Mhururu pa Basa*, which literally means ululating at work. The ululating at work is part of the Shona culture to encourage those at work to work harder. This was used mostly during the construction of the head offices. Circuits were called to give *Mhururu pa Basa*, which translates to being given an item to bring for the construction of the head offices. That initiative took the work to advanced levels.

The "Green Bishop" reflected environmental concerns and care. Each time we did some groundbreaking or the dedication of a building, the bishop planted a tree accompanied by other leaders present. Bring in the "Safari Mood," which came in as a promotional catchphrase. "The idea is to instill a spirit of readiness and action, action and little talk." This article gives a fair summary of what we tried to accomplish together with the people in the Zimbabwe Episcopal Area during my episcopacy.[9]

Strategic Plan

What the above article managed to capture was not all there was. For the first time in the history of the episcopal area, we organized and held a Strategic Planning Workshop over a weekend north of Harare. For a long time there had been talk of the need to have a strategic plan, but it all ended as talk with no tangible results. I shall forever give credit to those we assigned as leaders in putting together the strategic plan document. That document has provided clarity on the way forward for us in leading and supervising the church in Zimbabwe. The work of our strategic plan can be summarized as follows:

Vision and Mission Statement of the UMC Zimbabwe
The Zimbabwe Episcopal Area

VISION
To be a continuously transforming United Methodist Church in the Zimbabwe Episcopal Area, that claims higher ground spiritually, physically, and morally.

MISSION
The United Methodist Church in the Zimbabwe Episcopal Area is committed to making disciples of Jesus Christ through witnessing, outreaching, networking, and nurturing for the transformation of the world.

Common Pool

One of the nagging problems we have in the Zimbabwe Episcopal Area is inadequate support for the clergy. Their salaries are low. In addition to low salaries, we used to have situations where pastors went for months without even receiving the little due to them. This is a difficult environment for a bishop to run the church. We then decided to have what I call grand sharing. That is sharing among ourselves the little that we have. So, we created a Common Pool. A certain percentage from each charge is remitted to a central account, which is run by the Council of Finance and Administration, CONFAD, and monitored for distribution each month by the treasurer. It is encouraging to say that since the establishment of the Common Pool, our pastors are now able to share and get the little that might be available each month. The idea for the need to establish the Common Pool has been muted in the episcopal area for some years, but it did not take off for a number of reasons. I thank God that under my episcopacy, this became a reality.

Ebenezer Convention

The Ebenezer Convention has already been referred to in this chapter. I feel that it is still important to add some details to show how important this Ebenezer Convention was in the Zimbabwe Episcopal Area. Since the division of the annual conference into two in 2000, the people had not met together as one in their prayer time at conventions. In fact, the separation goes back even to the time when we were still one annual conference. From the time of the missionaries, people used to gather from all over the country for a camp meeting at a place called Nyatande in the eastern part of the country. Then later in the years two conventions were created, one for the south and one for the north. In order to keep a sense of togetherness, guest representatives were sent to either of the conventions. At no point had the United Methodists in Zimbabwe met as one family in one place for the purpose of prayer.

If we add the fact that in 2000 the annual conference was divided into two, you have a sense of separation drilled into people's minds. I observed these realities and concluded that it would be spiritually healthy if the people were to meet together in one place for a time of worship. I tested the idea in the Area Cabinet, and the district superintendents responded positively. For about two years I took every opportunity to talk about the need for such a convention at different meetings with the people throughout the episcopal area. I got a sense that the people were ready to embrace whatever it took for them to gather together for worship.

We did not know yet that we had started a process that was going to call for financial resources of considerable amounts, with numerous planning meetings for both the cabinet and various committees that were created for the purpose. The people were fully involved in doing whatever was assigned to them. In fact, the planning of the Ebenezer Convention gave me added confidence that the Zimbabwe Episcopal leaders from the cabinet to the clergy and the lay leadership were ready to rise to the occasion to implement what was needed. They led with creativity and determination.

From my point of view, that convention accomplished the following:

First and foremost, the convention made it clear that The United Methodist Church as a denomination was firmly established in Zimbabwe as a viable denomination among the others.

Second, the convention had both the spiritual and the psychological effects of saying "I am a United Methodist, it is good to see you too." In other words, by gathering together, they collectively confirmed their presence as one family.

Third, the convention fulfilled the African yearning of cultivating a communal sense of togetherness and fellowship. As I go around the episcopal area, I have gotten pleas for another Ebenezer Convention. One reason given is that, at the Ebenezer Convention, they were able to meet and visit with relatives they had not seen for a long time. If a church gathering can be a place where relations among families are renewed, there is nothing wrong with that.

Fourth, although not easily said, the convention had a positive side commercially for both the church and individuals. There was a carnival spirit that accompanied that coming together of the people. There was a lot of selling and buying, which benefited entrepreneurs in and outside the church.

Fifth, there was a feeling of goodness about everything that went on there. For the first time, it was good to hear voices from a mega choir that was put together. When they sang the "Hallelujah Chorus," it was amazing to hear how they were able to coordinate the numerous voices. The preaching itself was so inspiring. We had some of our partners who came to be with us. There was a good feeling.

So, the Ebenezer Convention was an event of the moment. It can be viewed and interpreted in many different ways, depending on the beholder. All to the glory of God.

Infrastructure

The United Methodist Church in Zimbabwe is still a growing church, and hence there is a constant need to provide shelter for the newly created circuits. Sanctuaries, parsonages, and other building for schools and hospitals are part of the requirements. I have labeled the Zimbabwe Episcopal Area as a building church. People still worship in makeshift structures for lack of resources to build decent churches. In some case, they walk long distances to access the nearest clinic. It is a common sight to see young children running to go to school long distances from their homes.

The episcopal area has done a lot in building churches, parsonages, and other buildings. In the context of chabadza, we have also joined hands with our partners to build some of the units. I shall say more about partnerships in the following chapter.

Head Office

In some cases, there was the need to improve on what we already had. In line with our strategic plan, we agreed that it was time we built new head offices, one in each conference, befitting who we are as a church. True to that vision, the people mobilized their resources and built the head office in the Zimbabwe West Annual Conference in Harare. Years later, the Zimbabwe East Annual Conference also succeeded in building a head office in Mutare. A lot is being said about these head offices as game changers in what the church was able to do in building such magnificent buildings. In Mutare, the head office building has made heads to turn in appreciation. It is an imposing building, which induces a sense of admiration.

The Zimbabwe East Annual Conference made the decision and voted to name the head office The Bishop Eben Kanukayi Nhiwatiwa Building. This humbles me. We dedicated this building on April 23, 2023. We thank God for such a collective achievement.

Teaching and Learning

The episcopal area has seen some tremendous developments in the area of teaching and learning, for both pastors and the laity. The laity instituted the Laity Academy. This is an annual event where the laity gather for teaching and learning. Every other year they meet with partners from the Western Pennsylvania Annual Conference at Africa University.

In the same vein, pastors hold their pastors' school every two years at Africa University in partnership with the Baltimore-Washington Area. These retreat learning times have done a lot by sharing skills that enhance our pastoral work in the area.

Spirit of Donations

There is an evident growing spirit in offering donations by families and individuals. Church members donate cars for use by the pastor at circuits. Others offer to contribute substantially in building churches and parsonages. This surge of giving donations is highly appreciated in the church.

Transport

As already hinted above, we now have a number of circuits that have managed to get donations or to buy their own cars for their circuits. This venture includes even rural circuits usually in the disadvantaged position in terms of resources. The men's and women's organizations have bought their own vehicles. The lay leadership has put in place the laity car fund for buying a vehicle each year to be given to a selected rural circuit. For us in the central conferences, where every penny used to come from the supporting churches of missionaries, this is a momentous development in line with the goal of self-reliance.

The Zimbabwe Episcopal Area has gone further by purchasing two vehicles for the bishop to use for different terrain. Such developments confirm the long-term positive outlook for the church.

Numerical Growth

While statistics don't tell the whole story, it is equally true that numerical growth that can be measured is so important. When I came in office as the bishop, the Zimbabwe Episcopal Area was allocated one clergy and one lay for each annual conference for delegates to the General Conference. That calculation gave the Zimbabwe Area a total of four delegates. Now the number has risen to two clergy and two lay for each conference. That gives Zimbabwe a total of eight delegates. Of course, this is still a very small number but it shows some movement in the numerical growth of the church membership.

Ordination of Pastors

One of the responsibilities of any bishop is to see that the church is well supplied with pastors. I can humbly say that the majority of the serving pastors in the Zimbabwe Episcopal Area at present have been trained and ordained under my episcopacy. When it comes to training of pastors, we are setting a high bar in the level of training. Zimbabwe can boast of a considerable number of pastors who have earned their PhDs, are in charge of circuits, and some are district superintendents. First-degreed pastors are so numerous, as well as those holding master's degrees. Just recently, someone asked to see who were Africa University alumni among the district superintendents; even I was surprised to see that a great percentage is from Africa University. The quality and level of leading the church attains high standards if those in leadership are well trained. It is therefore both the increase in numbers of the ordained elders and the attainment of university education that is important. In past years, university-educated pastors were few and far between

Ministries

A number of ministries take place in the episcopal area. One is the Ministry with Women. This ministry is so important in its work of spiritual formation through the conventions. Women are so visible in the work of the church. The men are not left behind. They are doing a lot in bringing others to Christ. The same goes for the youth. The young generation makes up the majority in the African countries. The church should ensure that the youth find a welcoming environment in the church.

Diaspora

The Zimbabwe Area has vibrant ministries in the diaspora: Dubai, UK Mission Area, New Zealand, Australia, Canada, and other areas. The United States has a Zimbabwe Women's branch, which is connected to the Women's Organization work back home in Zimbabwe. We find these ministries essential in keeping our people connected in worship

Malawi Provisional Annual Conference

Malawi is faced with numerous challenges of power struggles and the policies of the country, which has laws that are not germane to the way The United Methodist Church is organized and its polity.

A Number of Achievements

Some of the other achievements that we have made during this episcopacy include:

Maiden Trip to Israel

Our people used to tag along with others who had the numbers to arrange a trip to Israel. We finally managed to put in place our own trip to the Holy Land. Now it is a recurrent event that the church members and others look forward to. This is an important event in spiritual formation.

Hymnbook with Notations

Early in my Episcopacy, we entered into a venture of producing a hymnbook with notations. The hymnbook has done a lot in improving the quality of music, and the choir directors can now guide the people easily.

Braille Hymn Book

A braille hymnbook was put together, and we launched it a few years ago. Now our church members living with such a disability can have a way of participating in worship, blending well with the congregation.

Ndebele Hymnbook

A Ndebele hymnbook to cater to the Ndebele-speaking people, who are now joining The United Methodist church, is available.

Bishop's Scholarship

Through the initiative of the Episcopacy Committee, the two annual conferences agreed to raise funds to support two students annually at Africa University. They named that scholarship the Bishop's Scholarship.

The Cabinet

Let me conclude this chapter by touching on the cabinet. I find the cabinet to be one of the best structures of administration that the denomination has put in place. I relate to the cabinet in a variety of ways, such as coming up with possible initiatives for us to implement or receiving their suggestions about how to solve emerging challenges. We also discuss how we might improve our way of supervising the church in general.

Above all, the cabinet is critical in its responsibility of advising the bishop regarding the making of appointments and sending the pastors to different charges, as the district superintendents would have advised. I could not agree more with Bishop Jack Tuell, who wrote in his learned and inspired writings for the church, that the selection of the district superintendent is one of the most important any bishop could take.[10] The district superintendent is a central link in the chain that binds the connection. When it comes to the appointment of the district superintendent, I rely on the cabinet to make proposals and give advice, but the decision is mine in all respects. Early in my episcopacy, I surveyed the senior bishops in the Council of Bishops about what makes them select a pastor to be invited to the cabinet or to be a district superintendent. All of those whom I interviewed pointed to loyalty as the key component to be considered for one to be a member of the cabinet. You can teach anyone any skill, but you cannot teach one to be loyal.

I believe in the importance of orientation. I take time to orient my new district superintendents. I have written a manual for the training of the newly appointed district superintendents. In addition to the manual, I review other areas of church administration. Further, we take time in their first area cabinet meeting for the senior district superintendents to share their advice on how to supervise a district. In their regular reports to the cabinet, each district superintendent is expected to share some insights for sharing with the people. I have developed a form with a template on what should be reported on. This approach streamlined the way reports to the cabinet meetings were to given.

Each district superintendent is assigned a committee, board, or council and becomes a cabinet representative. The district superintendent is expected to attend the meetings of such an entity and come back to report to the cabinet. That way the cabinet is kept informed about what is happening in other sectors of the church.

We do have an Expanded Cabinet as well as what we call the Appointive Cabinet. An Expanded Cabinet brings in the chairs of selected committees or boards at a given time for them to update the Area Cabinet. The cabinet meets as an Area Cabinet. I changed from meeting each cabinet separately for the two conferences.

Tasks in districts are done by making arrangements within the Area Cabinet. I used to make a calendar for the whole year, but I changed since COVID-19 to quarterly calendars, which made it possible to adjust plans at short notice. For the cabinet to work in a productive manner, I found it important that there should be well-oiled horizontal relationships among themselves. As the bishop, I keep an eye out and ear to the ground to make sure that relations among the district superintendents are smooth and on the move. I have been fortunate to have good relationships among my district superintendents. They joke with each other and give each other free constructive advice.

I have intentionally created an atmosphere that encourages them to differ with me in good faith. They have learned that it is fine to advise me not to take a certain action and to follow their advice instead. I have also learned that they grow into the job. I therefore don't hesitate to counsel them on how things should be done, and they know that I am doing that for the good of us all and for the church above all.

From the very beginning I instilled in my cabinet that the words "not possible" will not be an acceptable answer to any situation. The district superintendents are aware that they could not come to the cabinet with unresolved problems. What we need is to hear about how they solved a perplexing problem instead of describing it. We look with disapproval at any cabinet member who wants to spend time giving us a litany of problems with no answers. It became clear to me that in the African context, if you accept excuses, then nothing will be done. There are so many reasons in Africa why something cannot be done. Therefore, the worst any leader can do is to hide behind excuses for failing to achieve.

Challenges

Challenges big and small, and even crisis situations, are part of leadership. I named one of my chapters, "Africa University Was My Crucible." The overall definition of a crucible is a complex, life-changing situation. In that vein, I regarded challenges as some form of crucible for me as a leader. I understood early that it was an unrealistic expectation to aim to be loved by everyone. Bishop Jack Tuell wrote in his book that "A bishop without enemies must not be showing up at the office."[11]

Sometimes challenges are generated so that you will be disoriented, frustrated, and then throw in the towel. This is why one's upbringing and general background is so crucial in leadership. One must be raised attuned to be able to face tough situations in life. My first chapter in this book has hints in that line. I like to see myself as a person made of stern stuff. We have a saying in Africa that a leader should wear the skin of an elephant when things get rough. When faced with a challenge or a crisis in my work, I make an assessment of the situation. What will be the worst scenario in such a situation? What could go wrong without recovery in such a crisis? When I get a clear answer, which in most cases is that nothing drastic will happen anyway, I realize that the challenge may have come as a way of testing how I would withstand the draconic situation.

General courage is very important for any leader. I found that if I were a person who bends to intimidation, it would have been difficult for me in my supervision of the church. Take every challenge as a crucible that must be faced vicariously and not be avoided. The approach is to remain calm and focused on your everyday work. Don't be distracted. Forward ever, backward never.

I am in the habit of reading military books. I have no idea whatsoever about the military but I get fascinated by the levels of bravery. Soldiers go out knowing almost daily, especially during war, that they might not come back to see their families again. But day after day, they go back into the trenches. Recently I have been reading the military ideas of Sun Tzu as applied to the field of leadership in business. These are some of the ideas which, when applied in my own way during challenges, see me through.

One very important posture to take in my situation in Zimbabwe is to always have the ground of operation well positioned for any crisis. You must be known, not too much and not too little, in government circles. When something happens, you don't want the leaders in the civil society to wonder, "Who is that person?" They must know you well. Do not be a stranger to them. To be able to know each other, converse whenever the opportunity allows.

For the rural areas, be a person known among the traditional leaders. Have them invited at church gatherings, especially when you the bishop are visiting their areas. Such groundwork will usually earn you support when challenges arise. You don't succeed all the time, but these are some of the ways that have served me well.

Conclusion

My episcopacy has opened new horizons in doing the work of God. I give credit to the leaders, both clergy and laity, for working together as a team. Most of what we have managed together has been possible because of the work of those who have gone before us, be they bishops, clergy, or the laity. Glory to God in the highest and peace on earth.

8

CHABADZA PARTNERSHIPS

Overview

Partnerships in the central conferences go back to the days of the era of missionaries. When missionaries came to Africa, they got support from their home countries. They were the ones who determined which projects were to be prioritized for fundraising. The focus of support was on the missionaries themselves before other considerations. When the missionaries itinerated on furlough, it was time to exhibit the dire conditions they were encountering in their work stations.

During the height of missionary activities, Africans exonerated themselves from supporting the church financially. One could come across reports at the annual conference in Zimbabwe saying that there was a need for a door at a particular church to prevent goats from entering the church. The congregation of such a church expected the missionaries to write to their home churches for money to buy that door. The Africans did not think at that time that they had any obligation to raise funds to maintain their churches. Church property was seen as "their property," meaning the missionaries. Missionaries were viewed as doing work for the Africans. Such an approach led to dependency syndrome, which is still a challenge in some areas to this day.

Funding of Ministries

The Board of Global Ministries, founded in 1940, was the center of mobilizing funds to finance ministries and programs in the central conferences. There was the Advance Special, which advertised projects from around the globe within The United Methodist Church that needed financial support. How quickly funds were raised depended on the interest a particular project managed to generate. The target churches to raise such funds were those in the United States. In the early years of the establishment of the Advance Special, enough funds were raised to build churches and parsonages.

As of now the Advance Special is no longer a major source of funding for programs in the central conferences. Sometimes a project is chosen but it fails to generate far-reaching interest in it. Funds collected will be very little for the expected budget. Many times, we renegotiate so that the designated funds might be channeled for use in other areas of need.

The Board is still helpful in the central conferences in funding the critical areas of need. When we were faced with the critical need of medical doctors in our areas, the board came forward and paid allowances to the doctors. We were able to keep our hospitals staffed. There was the millennium fund, which helped in the purchase of episcopal vehicles for the African bishops. This bishop inherited such a vehicle and used it for many years during my episcopacy.

Recently we have the Yambasu Agricultural Fund, which has given a kick-start to the agricultural ventures on our mission farms. The program has received considerable funding through the General Board of Global Ministries. The board has a facility to pay salaries to persons in mission (PIM). This initiative has helped central conferences tremendously. We were able to retain persons in critical areas of ministry through such a facility.

In the area of scholarships, there was the Crusade Scholarship, which was run through the Board of Global Ministries. A considerable number of people got higher education under the auspices of The United Methodist Church.

Paradigm Shift

Although the Board of Global Ministries is still playing an important role in funding initiatives in the central conferences, there are signs of a paradigm shift. The role of the General Board of the Global Ministries as a source of funding ministries in the central conferences is receding. During my time as bishop, I endorsed very few Advance Special requests. I have since stopped seeing any more of such requests.

The interest and attitude in supporting such programs is changing in the United States. It is likely that funding of programs was connected to those churches that had a history of supporting missionaries. It is now rare for a congregation to find reason why they should support a church in a remote rural area of Zimbabwe. It is now difficult to make a congregation feel emotionally connected to a situation in a far corner of the world.

There is a disconnect in a situation where the need of building churches is growing in Africa on one hand, and on the other hand, the number of churches closing is growing in the United States. To tell people in the United States that money is needed for bricks and mortar becomes a farfetched request. Interest to fund an initiative should be based on the visits to see for themselves what needs to be done. Congregations in the United States are now interested in creating relationships first before the talk about the need for financing.

Let me share some illustrations to make my point clearer. There are plans in the making between the East Ohio Conference and the Zimbabwe Area to establish a Laity Women's Institute. When I shared the proposal with Bishop Tracy Smith Malone about what that institute might look like, we were on the same wavelength. When we asked our people to meet and share what they expected that institute to be, there were divergent views. The East Ohio side emphasized that it was essential to first create a platform where the people will get to know each other. As one East Ohio woman leader put it, we need "to laugh together and cry together." The Zimbabwe side was thinking of funds to meet their needs such as building an early childhood development center and a girls' high school. They finally came to an agreement by patiently explaining to each other what each had in mind and how that need might be met.

The other example is an ongoing partnership with the Western Pennsylvania Conference and the Zimbabwe Areas. As I wrote this chapter, I had just given the go-ahead to Bishop Cynthia Moore-Koikoi and her leaders to invite the Zimbabwe team for a reverse immersion experience sometime in October 2023. The partnership covenant between the two areas has room for the people from Western Pennsylvania and those in Zimbabwe to visit each other for specific tasks in either of the two areas. Initiatives which call for funding of building projects will be going on side by side with the building of relations. The partnership that the Western Pennsylvania Area started during the episcopacy of Bishop Thomas Bickerton is enthusiastically being carried forward by the current bishop.

This is a dramatic change from what used to be the case during the missionary era. This need for knowing each other first before one could hear and know about project needs is growing. The recognition of these changes has led to a situation where conferences themselves, through their episcopal leaders, enter into a partnership. In some cases, a written covenant is put into place, as is the case with most of the partnerships Zimbabwe has with the other areas. The document establishes the agreed upon focus areas on which the particular partnership considers to be priorities.

Having observed the developments discussed above, it was necessary to create a sustainable way of sourcing funds for the development of the episcopal area and beyond. The approach of merely telling the people about the project you might have in mind for funding has become obsolete. It was then that I came up with the concept of chabadza.

Chabadza Defined

As described earlier in this book, *chabadza* is a term in the Shona language that denotes a cultural aspect connected with work. The practice is illustrated in the scenario of when you go out to do some work, such as cultivating the fields, you take an extra hoe, in case a friend or any passerby might come through your field. Instead of stopping the work, you just give the visitor the extra hoe for the visitor to join so that you work together. At the core of *chabadza* is the idea of working together instead of observing the other working alone. Further, *chabadza* is predicated on the assumption that the one who needs *chabadza* should be found working. If you are seen just seated in the shade under a tree, then friends and passersby will join and sit by your side. The person giving *chabadza* does not initiate the work to be done. The initiative rests with the owner of the field. The implication is that the one who does not work will not get *chabadza*. No work, no helping hand.

An important outcome of the chabadza partnership is that it eliminates the dependency syndrome. That mindset of expecting things to be done for you has no place in the chabadza partnership. For the approach to work, it was necessary to convince the two annual conferences in Zimbabwe that the chabadza concept was a viable and sustainable way of relating with those who wanted to partner with us. It was not easy to shift people from the established tradition of asking for an amount of money to build that church or parsonage with no preconditions. In the chabadza concept, we were saying, "Do something first before you can even think of finding a donor to fund your projects."

During the first quadrennium, I went around the area explaining the concept of chabadza as a way of finding partnerships in development. They had to shift from writing requests for funding from the Advance Special to a way of working together. The annual conferences heard episcopal addresses that urged and focused the delegates on the need for embracing chabadza in our area.

We shall turn to the Zimbabwe Norway Community Development Partnership as an example of the chabadza concept in action. Their write-up describes the role that I played in coming up with the vision of chabadza. "When Bishop Eben K. Nhiwatiwa came into office in 2004, he had a vision that The United Methodist Church should move away from the dependency syndrome and be a church in partnership with the outside world. With that vision Bishop Nhiwatiwa brought into the United Methodist Church the name "CHABADZA" which means working together."[1] Rev. Øyvind Aske, Norway General Secretary, noted that the point of "social holiness is very important. It is making us a church which preaches and talks about the word of God and demonstrates the same love with our hands, legs and resources. Social holiness is now being known through chabadza. It's something to be proud of because it's improving people's lives. May I again thank Bishop [Nhiwatiwa] for bringing this out."[2]

Anne Foster [Norway], Program Advisor, had this to say about chabadza: "I want to thank Chabadza for developing the communities and bringing people together across countries. It is very important and I would like to thank them for that."[3] In their own understanding of *chabadza* through engaging with communities, the Zimbabwe Norway Chabadza Partnership noted that "One of the core functions of Chabadza is motivating communities to engage in team work in development so as to promote sustainability of any given project."[4] Through chabadza, "We work with people, not working for the people."[5]

The reporter went further to note that "this then [chabadza approach] does not promote dependency syndrome but develops total community ownership and sustainability of the project."[6] "The program assists communities already implementing their own project. One of the most crucial factors in Chabadza programming is community ownership of the project which has proved to be the most crucial tool in projects sustainability. The concept of Chabadza was accepted, appreciated by all communities and is proving to be the best community strategy as far as capacitating local communities in developing themselves."[7]

Beginnings of Zimbabwe Norway Chabadza Community Development

It all started at a breakfast meeting where I was seated with Professor Roar Fotland, vice chairperson of Norway Board of Global Ministries. We were serving together on the board of directors of Africa University. At that breakfast I raised the issue of reviving and strengthening the partnership between the Norwegian United Methodist Church and its Zimbabwe counterpart. I acknowledged that Norway and Zimbabwe had a relationship that thrived during the era of missionaries. One of the known missionaries who became a household name in Zimbabwe was Rev. Kare Eriksson—"Baba Eriksson" or "Father Eriksson," as we called him. I went on to tell Professor Fotland that we were fostering a new approach in these relationships called chabadza. I explained that the core values of chabadza were working together as a team and community ownership of their initiatives. Working together and not working *for* the people becomes the critical aspect of the approach. As time was running out for us to go to the session of the board, Professor Fotland checked whether I was prepared to come to Norway and explain the concept that I had just shared with him.

I accepted the invitation with a grain of salt. How could the professor quickly decide to invite me to Norway to explain a concept I had shared with him briefly at a chance breakfast meeting, I wondered. I did not think that our conversation would lead to anything tangible.

Surprisingly enough, an invitation followed for my wife, Greater, and me to visit Norway in 2009, and in 2009, we found

Chabadza Partnerships

ourselves in Oslo, Norway. We visited both government offices and those of the church related to community development. The key people with whom I had served on the board of directors at Africa University, Rev. Tove Odland and Professor Fotland, were helpful in organizing the visit. The visit had an observable impact. "We have been working in partnership in development for a long time in other countries and it took time for them to understand but when you talked about chabadza in Norway it was appreciated in our church. Chabadza is now being talked about everywhere in Norway," according to Torill Langbraathen Norway Board of Global Ministries chairperson.[8]

Workshop in Zimbabwe 2010

In 2010 the leaders whom we had met with in Norway came to Zimbabwe. The purpose was to put in place the rules for implementation of the chabadza programs. What follows are some of the basic tenets agreed upon. What was emphasized was the need to work with the communities. The community should have the capacity to take full responsibility from planning through all the stages to implementation.[9] Local projects are required to have the following documentation in their files:

- A confirmation that a "development committee" has been elected in a democratic manner
- A simple project plan
- A project file where all the important documents are kept
- Account book consisting of cash book and voucher file
- Report format[10]

Some of the projects accomplished through this partnership include:

Educational Cluster

Chabadza revealed a known fact about the Zimbabwe people: they value education as the linchpin for development. Therefore, more projects were in education-related areas of development.[11]

Chikwizo Primary School

Chikwizo is in the Mudzi District. The community applied for assistance from chabadza to complete their primary School. Chabadza had an agreement with the Zimbabwe National Army. In that agreement the chabadza provided material such as river sand, cement, and bricks. The army provided labor. The local community provided the locally available material. "Chabadza extended to capacitate the community that working together is crucial in development work."[12]

Agriculture Cluster

The dip tank project in Nyamacheni is the first project under the chabadza development program in agriculture. Villagers were traveling long distances to have their cattle immersed to remove ticks, which carried diseases fatal to their cattle. A total of 1,549 households in twelve villages are served by the Nyamacheni dip tank in Gokwe.[13]

Chabadza assisted the community with materials not locally available such as cement and treated poles. The community provided labor, gathered the locally available material such as pit sand, river sand, and bricks. The community carried water from the Nyamacheni dam, which is 7 kilometers, using scotch carts. The dip tank saved cattle from the tick-borne diseases. Cattle are an important source of cash and livelihood for the people.

Health Cluster

Chabadza built a waiting mother's shelter at Nyamombe clinic in the Mutasa Nyanga district. In the absence of a proper and adequately furnished waiting mother's shelter, most mothers would have been forced to come to the clinic at the point of delivery, thereby increasing risk. Waiting mothers can now go to the clinic earlier and save lives.[14]

Transport Cluster

Chabadza worked with the community to construct the Chitora Bridge in the Zimunya communal area. One part of the bridge was swept away by the cyclone in 2000. The destruction of the bridge cut off the community from the school, clinic, church, and other service delivery amenities. The community sought assistance from The United Methodist Church through the chabadza program for the rehabilitation of the bridge. The people provided all the locally available materials such as river sand, pit sand, stones, and labor.[15]

These chabadza projects in all the above clusters are dotted all over Zimbabwe. What has been mentioned is just a sample from the many projects around the country. The benefit to the people is tremendous. Communities show their willingness to cooperate and express ownership by working together to provide the locally available materials. Chabadza Zimbabwe Norway has proved to be a major sustainable partnership in providing services beyond specific boundaries of United Methodist Churches in Zimbabwe. We now turn to partnerships whose work was confined directly to The United Methodist Church in Zimbabwe.

Partnerships with Annual Conferences

Chabadza partnership is thriving between the Zimbabwe Area and other various episcopal areas. With conferences we have projects like the building of churches, parsonages, church-related clinics and other projects under the umbrella of the church. Covenants specifying regulations to be followed are entered into.

Baltimore-Washington Conference

Zimbabwe has a formal chabadza partnership in development with the Baltimore-Washington Conference. During the time when Bishop John Schol served there, I was invited to speak about the chabadza partnership at their annual conference session. Following the sharing of ideas and the explanation of the chabadza concept, the two episcopal areas entered into a vibrant relationship.

The partnership between the Zimbabwe Episcopal Area and the Baltimore-Washington Area has two major components. There is the provision of assistance for the construction of churches, parsonages, and clinics. In all cases the respective congregations have to demonstrate the *chabadza* spirit by contributing substantially from what they are able to afford. In some cases, a congregation is expected to build up to roof level before any financial help might be expected. In other situations, they volunteer labor as well. The Baltimore-Washington Area and the Zimbabwe Area partnership has accomplished a lot in the area of church buildings.

The other component is for the training of pastors through the pastors' school. The covenant provides for a joint pastors' school to be held every other year at Africa University. The two area committees exchange ideas in planning the pastors' school. The team of selected pastors come from Baltimore-Washington and join hands with the Zimbabwean leaders and conduct the pastors' school. It is usually a phenomenal time to be together as the episcopal areas.

When Bishop Schol transferred from the Baltimore Episcopal Area, Bishop Marcus Matthews took up the partnership with equal zeal. Now the same commitment for this partnership has continued under Bishop LaTrelle Easterling. It is important to mention that the partnership between the Baltimore-Washington Area and the Zimbabwe Area goes back to the times of Bishop Felton May and on the Zimbabwe side to the times of Bishop Abel Tendekayi Muzorewa and Bishop Christopher Jokomo. What might have changed in my time are the added details of the chabadza component and the formal signed covenants.

Allow me some self-indulgence by taking the reader to an unforgettable blessed experience I had when I visited the Baltimore-Washington Area during the time of Bishop Schol. The arrangement was that after the annual conference session I was going to have lunch with Bishop and Eunice Matthews at their home. We left the venue of the conference with *Mbuya* Eunice driving. *Mbuya* is a word of honor in the Shona language, meaning grandma. The conversation between them along the way was of reminding each other about which turn to take. Of all the rides I have taken in my life, this one is forever etched in my mind. Anyone who knows who the Matthews were and the place they held in our denomination will understand what I mean. For me to be driven by *Mbuya* Eunice was a sacred honor of all times.

Western Pennsylvania

The chabadza partnership between the Zimbabwe Area and the Western Pennsylvania Area started during the time of Bishop

Thomas Bickerton. The chabadza partnership between these two episcopal areas has three components. First is the building of infrastructure, that is churches, parsonages, clinics, and the drilling of boreholes. Second is the Laity Academy component. As mentioned earlier in this book, the laity of Zimbabwe instituted a Laity Academy. Every other year the two areas hold a joint Laity Academy. The two planning committees work together. The team from Western Pennsylvania comes to Zimbabwe, and the Academy is held at Africa University. They were able to hold such an academy virtually during the times of the COVID-19 pandemic. We bishops are usually given some slot on the program to speak to the laity. Thus, Bishop Cynthia Moore-Koikoi and I participated at that online academy.

The third component of this partnership is the immersion. The immersion is an exchange visit by our people to each other's areas. If Western Pennsylvania members come to Zimbabwe, then the next visit will see those from Zimbabwe going on what we call a reverse immersion to Western Pennsylvania. At the time of writing this chapter, Zimbabweans will be on that reverse immersion visit to Western Pennsylvania. I have had the opportunity to visit the Western Pennsylvania Conference on invitation from Bishop Bickerton during the first immersion. Each immersion will have a program of selected tasks to be fulfilled. This could be in the area of sharing ideas on revitalizing the church, such as connecting church members through sections that resemble the tradition of class meetings. Zimbabwe is very good at that approach of bringing more people to Christ and nurturing them to stay committed. On a sidenote, during the first immersion we had among the Zimbabwe team a Zimbabwe judge, known by the title "Justice," as our conference lay leader. She had the opportunity to participate in the trial of a case in the court of law in Western Pennsylvania. These partnerships can produce contacts and relations beyond what one would have imagined.

A distinct feature about the Western Pennsylvania and the Zimbabwe Areas partnership is that there are designated people assigned to monitor the progress on the ongoing projects. There is a constant exchange of update reports from either area. Bishop Cynthia Moore-Koikoi and I have signed a renewed covenant for the partnership for some more years ahead. As bishops we demonstrated in faith that our people will forge ahead in their relationship irrespective of the air of separation engulfing the church in our times.

Great Plains Area

Zimbabwe has a chabadza partnership with the Great Plains Area, which started during the time of Bishop Scott Jones when it was Kansas East Conference. Greater and I visited the Kansas East Area to explain and demonstrate the concept of chabadza. The focus of the partnership is on helping in the building of church structures. A team from Kansas visited and toured the church in Zimbabwe. That was an important visit for familiarization among our people. Zimbabwean leaders have also visited Kansas East as an exchange visit. There is the pairing of districts in one area to the other.

Mississippi

During the time of Bishop Hope Morgan Ward, the Zimbabwe Area and the Mississippi Area entered into a partnership. It started with an invitation for me to come to the Mississippi Area after the devastating damage from Hurricane Katrina. Greater and I made numerous visits to churches and other areas in the episcopal area. We attended the annual conference, visited and stayed with church leaders in their homes. It was a time filled with joy and living memories, irrespective of the destruction that had taken place in some parts of the state.

While in Mississippi, the mayor of a town honored our visit by handing me the Key to Freedom of the City. We felt warmly welcomed in the area. Speaking of Freedom of the City, I gave Bishop Jonathan Holston the Freedom of the Pulpit when in Zimbabwe to arrange with pastors to preach at their circuits. The bishop comes to Zimbabwe most of the time in January. Those are times of making connections.

Bishop Hope Morgan Ward returned an invitation to visit Zimbabwe. She preached at the annual conferences and in churches. The youth from Mississippi visited Zimbabwe and painted a parsonage at St. John's United Methodist Church in Mutare. Whenever I pass through the St. John's UMC parsonage, I visualize those young people from Mississippi with their Zimbabwe counterparts joining hands to do some painting. The session I had with the youth was unforgettable. They had so many interesting questions for me about Zimbabwe and Africa in general. I hope that I satisfied their curiosity during their visit to Zimbabwe.

Other Partners

Some other partnerships exist, even though they are of a formal nature as explained in the cases above. There are connections between the East Ohio and the Zimbabwe Area. East Ohio is focused in the area of education. This relationship started back during the time of Bishop Jokomo. During my time we have hosted a team from East Ohio under the leadership of Bishop Tracy Smith Malone. They are currently focused on building a school in Matabeleland in the western part of the Zimbabwe Episcopal Area at Emsizini. This is an important focus because The United Methodist Church is still in the process of entering into the communities of the Ndebele people. When you build a school, you catch the attention of the parents. We now have a preaching point where the school is established, and other preaching points have been opened outside Bulawayo into rural Matabeleland. I have also mentioned the effort to establish an institute for the laity women of Zimbabwe and East Ohio Areas.

There are other groups doing a lot of work in the Zimbabwe Area. There are those supporting the Ishe Anesu at Hilltop in Sakubva Mutare. Then you have people, such as Mr. Charlie Moore of the community church in Baltimore, who are doing a lot of work especially in building schools in the Murewa UMP district. Charlie has integrated with the people of the Murewa UMP district to the extent that he is now known as *Soko Murewa*. The people of Murewa call themselves by their totems. *Soko Murewa* is the most common one. As soon as he steps on the Zimbabwe soil, forget about looking for Charlie Moore—you won't find him! Look for Charlie Soko Murewa instead. This is what the partnerships are doing in bringing people together. It is joy after joy in the midst of a lot of work to uplift the peoples' lives.

There is the Nyadire Connection which is driven by the interested group of supporters in the Western Pennsylvania Area. They have renovated clinics into modern facilities for the health delivery systems. At Nyadire they have improved the infrastructure there in many ways.

We have a group known as FOSA, drawn from different parts of the United States, focusing on the support of the Children's Home at Old Mutare Mission. Finland supports the Children's Home at Nyadire Mission. Children are vulnerable people whose lives depend on those who support these institutions.

Some conferences support the Children's Home in major ways by giving one-time gifts. We say thank you to all those. We should not forget some individuals who still regularly send contributions to various projects through the Advance Special, earmarked for Zimbabwe.

I might have left out some other people who have supported Zimbabwe in various ways; that is not intentional.

Accompanying Stories

These partnerships lead to memorable stories of friendship. You can ask Bishop Schol about the gift of a goat. We dedicated a church that the Baltimore-Washington Area had helped to build. In their expression of appreciation, in the Zimbabwe way, the people brought a goat for Bishop Schol. To resolve the challenge of how the goat was to be transported the United States, I assured the bishop that I was going to take care of it.

Bishop Bickerton is known in the Chitungwiza Marondera district as the "*Shanda* Bishop." *Shanda* in Shona means work, with the connotation of working hard. The people have turned it into a song "*Shanda, shandaa kushandira* Jehovah"—Work, work, work for your God. When it was sung, Bishop Bickerton picked it up and the atmosphere became vibrant.

With other bishops there were invitations to preach in their areas. This was the case with Bishop Ernest Lyght, when the bishop invited me to preach at his annual conference in West Virginia. It was a memorable occasion. I have the added opportunity of relating with a number of bishops on the Board of Directors for Africa University. This is true for Bishops Lyght, Matthews, Malone, Julius Trimble, Minerva Carcaño, Yemba, Carvalho, Gaspar Domingos, and John Kpahun Yambasu. The truth is that all of us bishops are connected through this beloved United Methodist Church.

With Bishop Hope Morgan Ward, we have kept these gracious contacts since our partnership during her episcopacy in the Mississippi Area. When she reads about some work done in Zimbabwe that catches her attention, she writes to give a word of appreciation. Recently she read about work of my wife, Greater, in leading the women in improving the location for prayer and devotion called Chingando at Old Mutare Mission. Bishop Ward sent a word of appreciation to Greater. As I write this chapter while in North Carolina after the Council of Bishops in Chicago April–May 2023, there are plans for a brunch with Bishop Hope and Mike at their home. God is gracious.

Bishop Rosemarie Wenner and Bishop Christian Alsted visited Zimbabwe at one point for the purpose of cultivating relationships. We say praise be to God.

There are many other uplifting relationships with other bishops that cannot all be mentioned in this book. Take, for instance, Bishop Jonathan Keaton, who whenever we met at the council, his greeting to me was, "Nhiwatiwa, Bishop of Africa." Or Bishop William Willimon who told me, "When I see you, all my problems are over!" Bishops Joaquina Nhanala, David Yemba, Daniel

Wandabula, and any other African bishop—we share a sympathetic expression, given the challenges we face in Africa as we supervise the church. Or it is Bishop Albert Fritz Mutti asking me through an email message on my birthday whether the family held a birthday party for me. What else do you ask for from a church that binds us together through these blessed contacts?

Conclusion

The chabadza partnerships will be the new way of sharing resources for development. While missionaries will still be needed in certain areas, the nurture of support has shifted. As we move forward, patterns of partnerships that encourage people to aim for more self-reliance will serve the church in Africa for a sustainable future.

9

MUKATI COUNCIL OF BISHOPS

The focus of this chapter from my own observation and experience is that the Council of Bishops is an entry point and process that makes every bishop feel welcome and like an insider. Let me start by explaining the term *mukati*. *Mukati* is a Shona word spoken in Zimbabwe that means "inside." There is an area of Zimbabwe, Mutoko Mudzi, which is rich in cultural practices. One of these is the practice of *mukati*. Before they greet a person, they give the person a cup of water. The idea is that they should not make you talk right away because you might be so thirsty that talking becomes difficult. Such a cultural practice should be understood in the context of the challenges of the lack of water. When the time to welcome you is due, then an announcement is made: *Mukati*! The greeting to make you feel comfortable and relaxed takes place. More so, *mukati* could be a call to people at the homestead that it is time for them to literally come inside for some crucial discussion or conversation.

For instance, when at the Council of Bishops there is a call to vote, a reminder is made that only active bishops will vote. According to this culture, the active bishops would have been called to come "*mukati*." It is the type of call given for the elders in a family to gather for some serious conversation related to them. The Council of Bishops plays that role for each and every bishop, and I will try to explain the process of mukati within the Council of Bishops.

Historical Background

The bedrock of mukati for any organization is to know the roots of that organization and what it stands for. It is therefore important to have some understanding of the historical background of the Council of Bishops. Before the 1844 General Conference, Methodists were one denomination, the Methodist Episcopal Church. Signs of divisions began to show long before 1844. The issues were complex, but all were interwoven with the different points of view over the power and authority of the episcopacy on one hand and the power and authority of the General Conference on the other.

As the gap between groups of people kept on widening, the church split into the Methodist Episcopal Church and the Methodist Episcopal Church South. Those in the North were in the Methodist Episcopal Church. The North favored the authority of the General Conference. The Methodist Episcopal Church South was for a strong episcopacy. Another issue that strained relations among the two groups was the issue of slavery. The North agitated against bishops and individuals who held or owned slaves. The South wanted to skirt the issue and carry on as if nothing amiss was happening.

There is always a straw that breaks the camel's back. In this case it was the issue of Bishop James O. Andrew, who was a slave owner. The General Conference of 1844 adopted a resolution that stated: "Bishop Andrew to cease to function as a bishop as long as he is a slave owner."[1] A committee of nine that had been formed and tasked to find a solution over Bishop Andrew's case reported that they failed to find any other way out of the issue. Instead, the committee went on to present "a contingent plan of separation" and sought some guidance from the General Conference. The question posed was whether "the annual conferences of the slaveholding states find the necessity to unite in a distinctive ecclesiastical connection." The report of the committee of nine became known as "the Plan of Separation." The authors of my source noted that the Southern historians record the breakup as "separation," while Northern historians call it "secession."

On June 10, 1844, a final vote was taken on the Plan of Separation with the results of 116 No, and 26 Yes. When it came to voting, the South always lost because they were few in number, whereas the North voters were in the majority. The only way out for Southern ones was to break away. As alluded to earlier, the Northern branch felt that the episcopacy should be subservient to the General Conference and not the other way around. They argued that the General Conference created the bishops who could be removed by the same conference. The South voters were of the position that they were bishops of the Methodist Episcopal Church and not the bishops of the General Conference. Bishops were the executive officers as well as the pastoral overseers of the whole church. The General Conference, on the other hand, was a representative unit of the church with limited responsibilities, the South argued.

The reason we have taken this long route is to get to the origins of the Council of Bishops. The precursor of the Council of

Bishops lies in the entities for the gatherings of bishops formed by the two separate branches of Methodism in America. The Methodist Episcopal Church South formed the College of Bishops. The Methodist Episcopal Church formed the Board of Bishops. It is important to note that an earlier break had taken place in 1830 because they were opposed to the strong episcopacy and also to the idea of including the laity in the leadership of the church. That break led to the formation of a denomination known at that time as the Methodist Protestant Church. This group became part of the negotiation for reunion in 1939.

Plan of Union

The Plan of Union had these salient features in it: the General Conference, annual conferences, the jurisdictional conferences, the Judicial Council, and the Council of Bishops. The Judicial Council "is the appellate tribunal of final authority in questions involving the constitutionality of legislative acts." The Council of Bishops "is the historic itinerant general superintendency constitutionally established and protected, charged with the specific duty of placing the ministers, presiding over the General Conferences, and supervising and promoting the spiritual and temporal interests and affairs of the entire Church."[2]

Bishop Nolan B. Harmon made clear the implications of the reality brought about by a formal establishment of a Council of Bishops in the new denomination: "This recognition and establishment of the Council of Bishops as an integral whole thus gives official status to a true General Superintendency which now inheres not in any one bishop but in the bishops organized as a Council.... To a certain extent this collective power of the bishops met with each other as individually to plan their work, and while they formed an organization of their own, their joint action was scarcely more than the sum of their individual might. . . . Now, however, in the Plan of Union, the Council of Bishops is recognized constitutionally, and to it frankly mandated Episcopal oversight over the whole church. It must and does exercise over the whole connection, its joint and complete superintendency."[3]

With this background it is now appropriate to look back at the process the Council of Bishops uses to bring bishops mukati, thus warmly welcoming them and making the bishops feel at home.

Orientation

There is an orientation session for the new bishops. As in any organization, an orientation is critical. It lays out expectations regarding a particular organization. The orientation hopefully touches on the workings of the Council of Bishops itself. It makes forays into what it means to supervise the church as general superintendents. Further best practices are highlighted regarding the supervision of the annual conferences.

I was fortunate to be able to attend an orientation session meant for the American newly elected bishops. The venue was the Simpsonwood Conference and Retreat Center in the North Georgia Conference. Much of the orientation was on advising the bishops on how to handle decisions of law that end up in the judicial council for a final determination.

In Africa we don't usually run into the need for a decision of law. One of the reasons is that the process is complex to lodge a question of a decision of law. The other reason is that to lodge a decision of law one has to identify him or herself and then sign the document. Africans are averse at taking processes requiring them to sign their names. The reasoning is that many Africans avoid an argumentative approach to matters of belief and faith. American society is a litigious one, which is now affecting the church. Having said that though, orientation plays an important role in bringing bishops mukati, inside of the general leadership of the church.

Faith Journeys

Another way the Council of Bishops uses to bring bishops inside is the sharing of faith journeys. The stories of faith journeys bring bishops to a common denominator based on the call to ministry. The stories could be as meandering as one wants, but it all boils down to, "Here I am Lord, send me." If the journey leads to the episcopal office, that is still fine but that is regarded as secondary. What matters is that these faith journeys level the ground for the bishops. It is like saying, "I am a bishop here like the rest of you." It is to highlight the essential point that the call to ministry is the foundation on which the episcopacy is anchored. Through sharing these faith journeys, every bishop enters mukati.

Covenant Groups

One of the most popular means of bringing bishops mukati are the covenant groups. I say most popular because evaluation surveys seem to indicate that covenant groups are viewed as among the most important ways of creating strong bonds of relationship among bishops. My observation is that in the covenant groups, bishops rarely spend their time talking about items on the agenda of the council. If anything, I have heard questions at the close of the covenant group, "Do you know what is coming up next?" I don't mean to say anyone will be belittling the agenda. It is only that there are times when human relationships take precedence over everything else. When the covenant groups were created in late 1990s, the purpose was "to help the ever-growing Council deepen collegiality."[4]

It is in the covenant groups that I have witnessed bishops exchanging jokes, smiling, or even laughing. The problem is that some of us from the central conferences miss the essence of some of the American jokes. If you can laugh at a joke, it means you are culturally mukati. Unfortunately, that does not happen too often.

Community Dinners

Community dinners get us out of the mode of a business gathering and turn it into a family center of oneness. No motions, no voting or anything of that sort, but a meal to be enjoyed. The challenge with most of us bishops, like many other people, is we find it difficult to wriggle out of thoughts about work. In fact, it was at these community dinners that the faith journeys were shared. One other important thing about the community dinners was that it was the precious time at which we were able to have a meal with our spouses. The Council of Bishops meeting at Chicago April–May 2023 was so good in giving us the opportunity to share some meals with our spouses.

Flexible Agenda

Let's face it, we bishops come to the council fully aware that it is time to work. But there is an unwritten agenda, private to each bishop: rest. It is a known fact that bishops come to the council after a last minute, hectic schedule in their episcopal areas. That is part of the joy of the job, of course. But it is daunting to overload the meetings with tight schedules. I don't know about others, but for me I found the schedule we had in Chicago excellent. It had adequate time for people to enjoy mukati by sharing and visiting of all sorts.

Presidential Address

The presidential address plays an important role in bringing bishops to be insiders. In the president's address, the president will be on display. Presidents do a lot of work out of the public eye in between council meetings. It is during the council meeting that the president becomes vulnerable before the eyes of peers. I for one feel so privileged to listen to what the president has to say. When you hear the official of an organization speak in your presence about the joys and the pains of an entity, it means that you are truly mukati.

Episcopal Address

The message of the Episcopal Address to the General Conference is crafted in the Council of Bishops as a sounding body. It is from within that address that the tone of the General Conference is hinted at. What a privilege it is for the bishops to have an idea about the highlights of an Episcopal Address before it is made public for the General Conference delegates. These are essential activities open to those who are mukati.

Memorial Services

Memorial services are important in the process of bringing bishops into the group of insiders. These services link new bishops to those who have passed on and who were active long before our time. It is so sobering and affirming to listen to and hear about what they were remembered for. The way bishops present those memories of the late bishops involve some art in speech making. The service is somber but uplifting through the hope of Resurrection. A quick look throughout the room will show an acute sense of attention, as if everyone is musing, *When will be my time to join this group of the faithful ones of God?*

Worship Services

It is a rare moment for a bishop to hear a sermon from another bishop. This happens at the Council of Bishops as if it takes place all the time. It is a glorious scene to watch as bishops file to different stations to receive Holy Communion. Irrespective of the different opinions and views, bishops become one family during those times of receiving one body and one cup. Communion has a way of binding people together. When I say goodbye to other bishops when parting from the Council of Bishops, I will be also be saying goodbye to these acts of grace, which filter through as we experience council work together.

Benefits from the Council of Bishops

There are different approaches one could use for the study of the Council of Bishops. One way is to assess what the council has achieved in terms of its focus at a given time. I did not want to take that route. There are minutes of the Council of Bishops and books written from such a perspective. I selected the mukati aspect as an important component in bringing the leaders of the church together. Now let us look briefly at what I have labeled the benefits from the Council of Bishops.

Call to Action

In the Call to Action the Council of Bishops provides leadership to the church at an appropriate time. When I take rounds in the episcopal area, I see the four focus areas displayed on walls in the offices of the district superintendents. The areas are:

1. Developing principled Christian leaders for the church and the world
2. Creating new places for the new people and renewing existing congregations
3. Engaging in ministry with the poor
4. Stamping out killer diseases of poverty by improving health globally

These four focus areas have been welcomed in my area, and they are the guiding format in their reports to the cabinet and in other arenas.[5]

Self-Care

I have benefited from the encouragement I get from the Council of Bishops on matters of self-care. I have instituted a component of self-care in the report format for my district superintendents. They have stretched self-care to include their housing preparations in retirement. From observing other bishops, I have tightened my exercise regime. This idea of self-care was part of the Council of Bishops from some years ago. Bishop Welch developed what is known as the Welch Quadrilateral as follows:

1. Moderate at work
2. Prohibition of worry
3. Trust in God
4. Little play along the way.[6]

Leadership

We have received opportunities of being refreshed in the area of leadership. Bishop Grant Hagiya and others have been tasked to arrange some learning sessions for the Council. We had professors from Harvard University taking us through the process of adaptive leadership, using books they have written. The Council of Bishops introduces me to some new concepts in leadership. *Liminal, pivot,* and the like are some mesmerizing terms that come to mind. Getting into these best practices is helpful for me.

Traditions Die Hard

Bishop Enoch George was in the habit of coming to the Council of Bishops and leaving almost immediately because he had to rush to another meeting. In 1826 Bishop William McKendree called for a meeting of bishops in his hotel room in Pittsburgh. The meeting lasted forty-five minutes and ended because Bishop George had to leave for another meeting. A second meeting was called and lasted even less, just thirty minutes. Again, Bishop George had to leave for some other important task. "Some bishops think, the Council is a waste of time and have more important agendas than the meetings; others come briefly and leave early, but the majority of bishops take seriously the disciplinary admonition 'The bishops share with other bishops for oversight of the whole church through the Council of Bishops," William B. Oden and Robert I. Williams observed.[7]

Conclusion

Let me conclude by citing Bishop Woodie White, whose presidential address fell in line with the mukati angle that I have taken about one of the major roles of the Council of Bishops. Bishop White had this to say in his fall of 1996 presidential address:

"How shall we hold each other up as Episcopal leaders—healing each other's hurts, hearing each other's cries, listening to each other's questions and ponderings? How shall we help each other be better bishops of the Church?"[8]

I personally commit myself to walk with the Council of Bishops, knowing that I am already mukati by the grace of God.

10

LEADERSHIP: A REPERTOIRE OF SKILLS

Overview

I view leadership as an eclectic discipline. A leader should be exposed to as many facets of leadership as is possible. I concluded that it was wise for me to read, observe, and be a perpetual learner in the arena of leadership. It was helpful for me to lead with a wide field of skills in leadership at my disposal.

While there are best practices tested through time, there are still situational demands on leadership. There is no one-size-fits-all in leadership. Further, different contexts require the application of selected skills to match the prevailing situation.

In this chapter I highlight those skills that proved to be most helpful as I supervised the Zimbabwe Episcopal Area of The United Methodist Church. Where possible, a skill, pattern, or style of leadership will be supported by an illustration to show how I used it.

Definition

The definition of leadership for our purpose will be multifaceted. I favor those definitions that are grounded in doing something. Leadership is about moving from theory to the concrete through action. Leadership is action-oriented. It follows that one of the main components of leadership is implementation. Without action and implementation there is no leadership. Leadership is about visioning in terms of seeing clearly a future direction. Rev. Zebediah Marewangepo, my former administrative assistant, used to tell a story about a group of people from another area of the country looking for directions. When they approached the Marewangepo homestead, the leader asked for directions. A family member asked the leader where exactly they were going, and the leader turned to his group and asked them where they were going.

This illustration might sound extreme, but the point remains that we need to know where we are going before we can lead others there. Ask each other about where you want to go as you craft the vision; when you have the vision, you can then embark on the journey.

My favorite description of what leadership is comes from the elements of adaptive leadership. As the Council of Bishops, we had the privilege of having Professor Marty Linsky speak to us on adaptive leadership. He and his colleagues authored a book, *The Practice of Adaptive Leadership: Tools and Tactics for Changing Your Organization and the World.* Adaptive leadership is summarized in three key activities:

- Observing events and patterns around you

- Interpreting what you are observing (developing multiple hypotheses about what is really going on)
- Designing interventions on the observations and interpretation to address the adaptive challenge.[1]

Adaptive leadership is "an interactive process involving the three steps which require the leader to: observe, interpret, and intervene."[2] Apart from routine processes, much of what I found myself doing in supervising the church involved these processes in one way or the other.

Another aspect of leadership is about having influence. You have to be believed, and then people follow. To lead means having those who are willing to follow your guidance or advice.

Leadership involves decision-making. One takes action after a decision is made. When we met as the Area Cabinet, there were a number of actions that needed to be decided on. At the end of the meeting, we checked on the action items. These action items were the ones that needed to be implemented. And there was follow-up if a separate group was implementing it.

When people talk about leadership, there is a tendency to overlook the routine. It is an important part of leadership to be aware of the things one has to do. The routine level appears to be mundane, and yet if ignored, the vision itself might be impaired. Aspects of leadership are interconnected. Take the adaptive leadership with its key activities of observing, interpreting, and intervening, and then consider this statement: "The essential function of Episcopal leadership, challenges the Council of Bishops to keep its eyes wide open."[3] To keep eyes wide open leads to the activity of observing so as to be able to interpret and intervene.

Leadership in The United Methodist Church

Under the heading "Nature of Superintendency" in the 1980 *The Book of Discipline*, some concepts of leadership are delineated. For The United Methodist Church, the task of superintendency "resides in the office of bishop and extends to the district superintendent, with each possessing distinct responsibilities."[4] I go further when orienting my new district superintendents, that they carry out all those responsibilities in a coleadership position of leading the church together.

Guidelines for Superintendency in This Age.

"The demands of this age on the leadership of bishops and district superintendents in the United Methodist Church can be seen in mode, pace, and skill."[5]

Mode

By *mode* we are referred to the way of doing things regarding leadership in an acceptable pattern and using best practices: team building for consensus-oriented leadership, ability to listen and declare the prophetic voice, nurturing the spirit of negotiation, and anchoring all forms of leadership in the spiritual disciplines.[6]

Pace

This is the rate at which work is done. In today's language, *pace* means agile and nimble.

Skill

I take skill as a display of one's area of expertise. That is the area of leadership one knows and feels comfortable in executing. Spiritual discipline is one of the areas of interest for a church leader. All the knowledge and effort should focus on bringing people to Christ.[7]

Servant Leadership

The United Methodist Church espouses servant leadership as the main feature in leading the church. Leaders in the church are expected to look to Jesus as their model. It is about "washing people's feet." I like the expression when commissioning district superintendents where the ritual emphasizes that one comes not to be served but to serve. It is a life of service to the people. There are privileges and obligations. The privilege lies in the call to form congregations, while the obligation is the call to form Christian discipleship.[8]

A Wide Range of Skills

Planning

I give a lot of attention to planning. I work better if I have a clear outline to follow. Without a plan you open yourself to other people's agendas about what should be done. I used to plan my calendar for the whole year and followed it successfully. The COVID-19 pandemic changed all that. I now plan quarterly calendars in order to be more flexible. Planning has its rewards. In his book *Eat That Frog!* Brian Tracy says, "The good news is that every minute spent in planning serves as many as ten minutes in execution."⁹ The author referred to what he called the Six P Formula, which says: "Proper Prior Planning Prevents Poor Performance."¹⁰

Emotional Intelligence

Emotional Intelligence is a skill that is highly rated in leadership. My experience with this skill is that it should be embedded in one's personality. It is a skill that should accompany the leader on every path of the leadership journey on a daily basis. I have had numerous situations where certain behaviors at the annual conference were deliberately designed to be provocative as a way of derailing my attention. If you lose your head before the people, you have lost their respect. There is a story intended to convey some wisdom. It is said that if you go out to bathe at a river in the open and a mad person comes by and takes your clothes, if you run after the mad person, people will blame you as the most mad person they have ever seen. The teaching is that the mad person is already known in the community as mad anyway. Yours is to stay in one place until some help comes. I thank God that in most cases the mature side of me takes charge. "Emotional intelligence is the sine qua non of leadership."¹¹

Visioning

We have touched on visioning, but it is necessary to give this skill more attention. Visioning is a crucial skill that I use regularly. Early in my position as the episcopal leader, I envisioned that we needed to take the episcopal area a step further from where our predecessors left us. As stated in the book already, we developed a strategic plan. One of the major features of that plan was that we were to build modern church head offices. We succeeded in building two church headquarters, one in each conference.

Another piece of visioning among many is the concept of chabadza, which has been described fully in the chapter on partnerships. It was a game changer in that we jettisoned ourselves from merely asking for financial help without us committing ourselves in doing our part.

Courage

I don't understand courage in the sense of not fearing something that might cause harm. For me, courage for a leader means standing firm so as to encourage people that they are able to do what may look like an impossible task. Courage means being a principled leader who does not change for self-seeking interests. When intimidating situations arise, courage demands that the leader remains calm and exudes confidence before the people. It is important to remain focused in times of confusion. You cannot remain calm if you are not courageous. Sir Winston Churchill is credited with saying that "Courage is rightly considered the foremost of the virtues, for upon it all others depend."[12]

In his book, Tracy went on to observe that "The difference between the brave and the coward lies in that they are disciplined. The brave person disciplines himself to confront, deal with, and act in spite of the fear."[13] Crown these views on courage with President Franklin D. Roosevelt's clarion call: "The only thing we have to fear is fear itself."[14]

Time Management

I have succeeded in projecting an image of one who keeps to the set time on events. When I became the bishop, I started by instilling in the cabinet a sense of keeping to time. Some of the cabinet members thought that I was not going to walk the talk. They later found out that if they arrived late, we were not going to brief them on what had transpired. On one occasion I arrived at the point of dedicating a parsonage, and the district superintendent was not yet there. I told the pastor that we needed to proceed. The pastor did not know whose instructions to follow, mine or the district superintendent, who was his immediate supervisor. I noticed that the pastor was hesitating. I told him that I was acting both as his district superintendent and his bishop, and so the work proceeded. The district superintendent arrived when we were about to receive the benediction. We then proceeded together to the next dedications. Consistency matters if people are to take you seriously.

I do my tasks ahead of time. I don't work well under pressure, so I give myself adequate time to accomplish the tasks at hand. Sam Silverstein in his book explains, "The most critical commodity that you have as an executive or as a CEO running a business is your time."[15] Another author discusses The Law of Forced Efficiency that says, "there is never enough time to do everything, but there is always enough time to do the most important things."[16]

Adaptive Leadership

We have already discussed the tenets of adaptive leadership in the overview of this chapter. I only need to share some practical experiences in using this approach. Adaptive leadership worked so well for us in the Zimbabwe Episcopal Area during the COVID-19 times. We did almost everything we needed by being able to adapt to the prevailing situation. We did most of our ministries virtually, even commissioning new district superintendents virtually. We brought in new members of the women's organization, Rukwadzano Rwe Wadzimai, in diaspora by conducting the ceremonies virtually.

One of the most important activities we did was connecting the Zimbabwe United Methodists throughout the world in a memorial service for those who passed on through COVID-19 or from any other disease. It was awesome to see candlelights showing on the screens of computers. Messages of comfort were preached. Up to this day our people talk about that service with appreciation.

Change

A lot of change has taken place. I have already mentioned the change we adopted when doing groundbreakings and dedications. Groundbreakings were done on weekdays, and only the dedication of churches took place on Sundays.

The days for the annual conference session were reduced. During the COVID-19 pandemic, we started the annual conference session on Saturday morning and finished all business. We then did the ordination on Sunday following. There were many more changes we undertook.

Creativity

I am averse to monotony. I love to see some effort in creativity. Bring out the new in everything. Previous chapters in this book have made reference to the bishop of many names reflecting on the programs we engaged in. The announcements of those programs were made in a creative manner. "Usu Ku Usu," instead of saying I was planning to visit the people in their circuits. "Maziso Pasi, Maziso Mudenga," that is, seeing everything, instead of saying I was visiting to inspect how things were at the institutions.

That would have intimidated the people. But with Maziso Pasi Maziso Mudenga, they anticipated the same inspection without attaching negative thoughts to it. Instead, they were so excited to welcome their bishop.

Presiding

Presiding is one of the responsibilities of a bishop. In the early days I became tense and uncomfortable. That has changed. I now preside with ease in a relaxed posture, accompanied with some expertise from experience. I had the privilege of presiding at the General Conference session in Portland, Oregon, in 2016. It was a memorable time for me, presiding at the highest church conference in the denomination. The reader might be surprised to know that the part I liked most about that act of presiding was when I announced and directed the delegates to "Vote now," when in reality I was not sure whether I understood what they were voting for. Lord, have mercy.

Confidence

According to Tony Schwartz, "Confidence equals security, equals positive emotion equals better performance."[17] There are prerequisites for gaining confidence. Avoid self-defeating mentality, don't declare success too early, no blame game, no defensiveness, anticipate setbacks.[18] Confidence is not a one-time accomplishment. One has to continue working on it until it becomes part and parcel of one's disposition.

Political Savvy

People are not comfortable admitting that there is a lot of politics and politicking in the church. Most, if not all, organizations have their own politics. If there is a kitchen at your working place and you have to ask for the keys from the custodian in order to get in there, that is politics. It is politics in that even I as the bishop must recognize the power and authority of the custodian in deciding when and to whom the keys are to be given. The moment you begin to figure out how you might influence the course an impending event, then you are involved in politics. The point is not how to do away with church politics, but how the work can be done with a humane heart. In his book *Leadership,* Michael Heath asks a rhetorical question: "Why is it some leaders perform all their functions well, yet make little impact in their organization?" He offers an answer: "One of the reasons is that they lack political savvy and don't appreciate the underlying informal power dynamics that influence the success of key initiatives."[19] Heath went on to suggest what those who are good at organizational politics do. First, they are aware of what they are not able to control and conversely can control. Second, they are good at timing and hence take action at the right time. Third, they have some insight in knowing who is with them and who is against them. He also makes the point that you might not do anything differently, even if you know what organizational politics entails. The important thing is to know that your organization has some political inclinations at one time or the other.

Delegate

In The United Methodist Church, the structures of the church are set up in a way that make them amenable to delegation. I added my own structures to strengthen the existing ones. Delegation is not a way of abandoning one's responsibilities. When done well, delegation gives you an opportunity to be involved in every aspect of what might be going on in the church at any level without your being there in person. Those who are delegated to carry out some tasks should be oriented to know what they are expected to do.

Take the cabinet, for instance. That unit of leaders was put in place as a hub for the bishop to delegate to as much as the bishop sees fit. The role of the district superintendent is a delegated responsibility. I introduced a system where every district superintendent is what we call the cabinet representative. Each committee, board, council, and organization has a cabinet representative. These cabinet representatives bring reports to the cabinet. In that way, the bishop and the cabinet are kept abreast about development in the area at large. In addition, there is the administrative assistant to the bishop. The administrative assistant is the one who chairs most meetings and oversees the other areas. I usually chair only those meetings that might require policy making involving other leaders outside our church or from outside the boundaries of the conferences. I have instituted the office of deputy administrative assistants to lessen the burden of the administrative assistant himself.

Timing

For timing to work out well, I observed that I needed to be clear in my own mind about what I wanted the people to buy into. There is the need to listen carefully to check whether people might be saying anything related to what you are focusing on. In the African culture, people gather and visit spontaneously without any appointment or prior arrangement. It is in those gatherings where critical information might be passed or ideas about certain issues are shared. As I worked on this chapter, we had experienced a number of deaths in the church. I noticed that our laity and the clergy were moving up and down, comforting each other tirelessly. At one of the funerals, I took the opportunity to announce off the cuff that we needed to train our laity on how to comfort and counsel each other in time of bereavement. I noticed that this announcement was well received, even though it was a time of mourning. Timing was proper because they were in the actual experience of an event of grieving.

Handling Stress

There are more stress-inducing jobs than ever before. Episcopal leadership is among those stressful jobs. By chance I met a bishop of a different denomination. He had in his company an older man, a layperson. After exchanging greetings, the man asked, "Are you a bishop too? Before I even replied, he went on, "That's a difficult job!" Well, the other bishop and I just giggled. But the point was made that even the one observing from the side did not miss the essence that it is a difficult job. It is doable, though. That is why it is important to know and have skills of how to reduce stress. One of those skills is the one we have just discussed: delegation. Don't try to do everything. Know that work will always be there; you can never finish it all.

I was surprised when I read a book that the United Methodist women bishops wrote based on their individual and collective experiences. At one point in the process of gathering information, the conversation went as follows: "What the episcopacy and the ordained ministry have done is push me from optimism to hope. And what I mean by that is that I've seen more clearly in the [episcopacy] role the underbelly of the beast. And it is not pretty. And yet out of that is how I can hope."[20] The other one responded, "It didn't slay you." The response came, "And we haven't slayed it, but we stand in the midst and offer alternatives to [the beast]. The kind of community we have been talking about is an incredible antidote to the beast."[21]

But the beast remains a matter of concern as it is suspected to be causing health issues among the women bishops. Coming from my reading in another book, the conversation went on, "There's another dimension. I don't want us to lose sight of the fact that a lot of us have had cancer. I believe there's a correlation between our journeys and our health. I believe there's a correlation with the cancer we've had with the journey we've taken."[22] In addition to the challenges of episcopacy itself, women bishops are faced with other issues that complicate their role as bishops in The United Methodist Church. In their case, stress is not only related to the responsibilities of the episcopal office; it goes beyond that.

How do we handle stress? There is no definitive answer to that. While dealing with cognitive health, what Patrick Gilkey and Clint Kilts write about in their article on cognitive fitness can be applied to stress reduction processes The two authors emphasize working hard at play. They said that the origin of the word *play* in Old English is "plegian," meaning exercise. "As you go about the hard work of your career, it is critical to remember to play."[23] The authors note that "play is a tool that we must consciously use, as the demands on us increasingly call for greater levels of emotional control but as we get older, we unfortunately tend to play less often."[24]

Another critical skill in handling stress is "adaptive capacity," defined by Warren G. Bennis and Robert J. Thomas as "applied creativity—an almost magical ability to transcend adversity, with all its attendant stresses, and to emerge stronger than before."[25]

Alia Crum and Thomas Crum came up with the view that stress can be good. They argue that it is normal to stress under some situations. One could stress when working on a difficult project but at the end there will be joy.[26] Some stress should be intentionally endured. Simply reframe your response to stress as something beneficial to you.[27]

Integrity and Character

A person of integrity and good character can go a long way in being an acceptable leader to the people. People can tolerate lapses in other areas but not failure in integrity and character. According to Silverstein, "The core value of character is truth."[28] Integrity is at the center of character. "It is your level of integrity, living in complete truth with yourself and others, that demonstrates more than anything else the quality of your character."[29]

Resilience, Staying Power, and Stamina

All the power traits boil down to pointing out that you are not a pushover-type of person. I discovered that true leadership needs some challenging situations now and then. Leaders become reinvigorated during crisis times. Everything is tested during those hard times, be it agility, adaptive ability, action, wisdom, courage, and you name it. All these skills and much more are needed.

Prioritize

Some skills are interchangeable. You cannot talk about prioritization without implying that you care about how you use your time. Again, Brian Tracy has something he calls "the Law of Forced Efficiency." We have already come across this idea about how to use a scarce commodity: time.[30] "To set proper priorities you must set posterities as well." Tracy defines a priority as something that one does more often and sooner. A "posterity" is something you do on an irregular basis and later.[31] Setting priorities is a strategic skill.

Strategic Intent

Strategic intent represents everything a leader stands for. Strategic intent, writes Silverstein, "is the driving overriding goal that motivates and empowers you. On the individual level, it helps one to be at a level of excellence at all times."[32]

No Excuse

The "no excuse" idea is something my cabinet members are well aware of. The mantra is that there is no room for an excuse for not being able to do anything. No is not an option. Excuses are ways of avoiding facing reality and addressing whatever the challenge might be.

Discipline

Whatever one does must be undergirded by discipline. Lack of discipline is what differentiates winners and losers. Lack of self-discipline is behind most failed plans.[33]

Leadership Fitness

Leadership fitness is a skill that says that a leader must be a perpetual learner so as to keep abreast with what might be new in the arena of leadership. Continue to cultivate all aspects that make you an excellent leader. Observe, take opportunities for learning, seminars, reading books, and whatever comes your way. I am in regular attendance of the seminars held in Johannesburg under the Institute of the Future of Knowledge. The institute is led by my former student who is a professor there. I am on the list of those to be invited whenever they have a virtual public lecture. It is a great opportunity for me. I get to meet and connect to professionals who are far from my colleagues in the regular work of the church. To my surprise, they seem honored to know that I, the bishop, am connected to listening to their presentation. But I learn a lot and apply some of the principles to work as I supervise the church.

As I watched TV during COVID-19, I took the opportunity to learn from the world leaders on how they were trying to mitigate the impact of the pandemic in their countries. There was on display a variety of leadership skills. Learn and observe from anywhere. As Adriaan Groenewald stated. One must "do what is necessary to fall in love with leadership."[34]

Self-Care

As I mentioned in an earlier chapter, one of the lessons that I learned from the Council of Bishops is self-care. A number of bishops engage in exercise. I got inspired when they came to breakfast in their exercise gear. Exercise is a way of life that I had already adopted long before I became a bishop. The idea is to remain active, involving moving the body more. I have introduced a section of self-care for reports to the cabinet as a way of reminding each other that an aspect of the job is to keep fit as much as possible.

Conclusion

Leadership skills come in different forms, all for the purpose of improving how we lead. It looks like we are still continuing to learn about what it is that people are looking for in leadership. I found numerous best practices that served me and the people so well in my leadership career. Still, if I come across a book on leadership, I still get hold of it as if I have no idea about what leadership is. When it comes to reading, I have immersed myself in the *Harvard Business Review* and other sources. There are many more skills and patterns out there that could not be included in this chapter because of space limitations.

11

TRANSITION AND RETIREMENT

Overview

This chapter is in two parts. The first part will deal with transition focusing on the Zimbabwe experience, detailing how the episcopal office in Zimbabwe has changed hands.

The transition segment will include the report of the Central Conference Committee on Episcopacy. What the 2016 Africa Central Conference agreed to implement will take the central conference to a new level of conducting episcopal elections in its area of jurisdiction. There will be reference to the expectations agreed upon at the 2016 General Conference. At the time of writing, there were indications that the budget to be presented at the 2024 General Conference will have major cuts in it. It is still a wait-and-see situation about whether the five additional bishops that were passed can still be possible. The separation in the denomination does not bode well for the needed budget to accommodate those additional bishops. But as I have indicated, it is the General Conference with a final say as it meets in 2024.

The second part will be on the prospects of my retirement as originally envisioned and where we are in that process. There will be a sharing of views about how I envision my retirement. Some research findings will enrich this part as might be necessary. Retirement will be discussed within the context of African culture, with the village life of Gandanzara highlighted as an example.

Definition

Transition entails change. It is a process of changing from one stage to another. One can see transition as a movement, development, a paradigm shift in the course of time. Beyond this definition we should embrace transition in the wider context of change. "Nothing is as permanent as change," says Dr. Myles Munroe.[1] "Change is both evidence that we are alive and proof that we are finite—because everything has its own season and nothing on this earth lasts forever."[2]

When we go through transition it is helpful to understand where we stand as individuals. The four categories of change which Munroe puts forward are: "(1) change that happens around us, (2) change that happens to us, (3) change that happens within us, and (4) change that we make happen."[3]

Processes

For a smooth transition there is need for thorough planning. In the church a combination of committees such as the episcopacy committee, Council on Finance and Administration (CONFAD), and Board of Trustees have been useful for us in Zimbabwe. In any organization, the church included, transitions take place in one way or the other. It goes without saying that leadership transitions are critical. But leadership transitions can be complex and lead to uncertain times.

Komal Gulati has identified some strategies that could be helpful in avoiding pitfalls in the process of leadership transitions. These are:

1. Let go of previous roles. Participants should adjust and align themselves to the new roles.
2. Embrace new relational dynamics with old colleagues. One way is to encourage collaborative approach among the leaders.
3. Manage stakeholders. The new leader should adapt to the new environment and remain focused. Take an active role to assume the new responsibility of providing leadership to the stakeholders.
4. Offer leadership coaching and development. Make sure that the new leaders are fully oriented to the existing culture and values.[4]

"Without structure or on boarding mechanisms in place, it's easy for new leaders to feel lost," Gulati goes on to say. "A seamless leadership transition does not happen overnight but it is possible to create a smooth change of guards. A new leader must maintain balance, be consistently self-reflective and remain engaged in the day-to-day of their new role."[5]

Approach

The transition from one bishop to another has not been without hiccups, so to speak. I will recall our recent heritage of the transition The United Methodist Church has experienced in Zimbabwe. As already noted, we will also go through the guidelines or policies that the Africa Central Conference put in place to help our areas to have smooth episcopal transitions at its 2016 session in Luanda, Angola.[6]

A Tale of Three Episcopal Transitions

From Bishop Dodge to Bishop Muzorewa

Bishop Ralph Dodge was elected to the episcopacy in 1956 to serve the church in Mozambique, Angola, and Zimbabwe. He was reelected in 1960. In 1964 the Ian Smith regime deported the bishop and sent him into exile to Zambia for his outspoken views on racism and other political issues. In that same year in August, the Africa Central Conference met in Congo and Bishop Dodge was reelected. He had to administer the church in exile for the next four years.

After the Uniting General Conference of 1968, which gave birth to The United Methodist Church, the Africa Central Conference met in Botswana for its business. Bishop Dodge came from Zambia to join his delegation from Zimbabwe. When the Zimbabwe ballot came up, Bishop Dodge was reelected. Soon after the announcement that Bishop Dodge was reelected, the |bishop himself stood up to announce that he was retiring and that someone else should be elected for the episcopacy in Zimbabwe. Here is what Bishop Dodge wrote in his book *The Revolutionary Bishop Who Saw God at Work in Africa*: "I was again re-elected on the first ballot but, knowing the impossibility of serving effectively any longer, I announced my retirement."[7] In a well-planned episcopal transition, the retirement of Bishop Dodge would have been widely known in advance both in The United Methodist Church in Zimbabwe as well as in the Africa Central Conference. Because of the prevailing circumstances, that was not to be. Bishop Dodge made an observation that plans for his successor were not well planned.[8]

For us to have a deeper understanding and appreciation of the extent of the challenges that the church in Zimbabwe faced at the time, let us turn to Bishop Muzorewa. In his book *Rise Up and Walk*, Bishop Muzorewa wrote, "Balloting started the morning of August 28. As expected, Bishop Dodge was re-elected bishop on the first ballot." Bishop Muzorewa went on, "Also as planned, the bishop immediately announced his retirement. Balloting continued for his successor until after the sixth ballot when the presiding bishop announced: 'Number of voting seventy. Number needed for election fifty-three. Rev. Abel Muzorewa received fifty-six votes and is elected bishop.'"[9]

Come on now. My disposition on this matter tells me that, when the delegates left Zimbabwe for Botswana, either all or some knew about the "plan" that Bishop Dodge was to be reelected just for protocol to show respect for him and save face. We ask again what was known and unknown by the whole church in Zimbabwe about these predetermined events and processes in the episcopal transition. Here you have an episcopal area that was making a phenomenal leap from the White missionary episcopal leadership to the first African bishop. This historic transition was taking place in a haphazard manner because of the circumstances beyond anyone's control. This is also about the African culture, which says that in difficult times things about leadership should be privy only to the selected few elders of the family or an organization like the church. The rest of the people will know as events unfold. Bishop Muzorewa took note of the magnitude of the transition. "As the conference drew to a close, I felt the heavy responsibility before me as leader of our United Methodist Church and the first African head of a major denomination in Rhodesia."[10]

To show how abrupt and stressful this transition was, we turn again to Bishop Dodge. "The Conference presented Eunice and me with a beautiful silver tea service, the engraved tray read: 'Presented to Bishop and Mrs. R.E. Dodge for faithful leadership and service to the Methodist Church. Rhodesia Annual Conference 1956–1968.'"[11] Just in passing, we can conclude that it was not a last-minute thoughtful gift with all the engraving. It had been prepared long before they arrived in Gaborone, Botswana. Further in his memoirs Bishop Dodge wrote: "We rode the bus from Gaborone to Francistown with the Rhodesian delegation. As I could not cross into Rhodesia, we bid them and their new bishop farewell, and waited for a plane to take us back to Zambia."[12]

Even as we are separated by the long mental distance created by the passage of time, we can still recreate an emotional terrain submerged in the quagmire of anxiety and confusion. In turn Bishop Dodge could not bid farewell to the church whose congregations he visited, be it at Zaranyika in the Murewa UMP, Chitekwe in Mutoko Mudzi, or in the valleys and hills of Rupinda in Mutasa Nyanga. Indeed, we all wish for better transitional times if and when the situation permits.

From Bishop Muzorewa to Bishop Jokomo

Given the period we are focusing on, the transition from Bishop Muzorewa to Bishop Jokomo was spared the hurdles we have just narrated. The church knew that Bishop Muzorewa was going to retire in 1992. There was no hide-and-seek about it. There was ample time for the church to be adaptive to that reality. We celebrated the transition joyfully because the leaders had planned for it.

From Bishop Jokomo to Bishop Nhiwatiwa

Then our bishop fell sick. For those who knew him, you can vouchsafe with me that in Bishop Jokomo we had an intelligent and wise leader. He was nimble and agile at everything he put his mind and hands to. His bar of performance and organizational skills was set so high to the levels of proficiency and excellence. All that was gone in the snap of a finger as a result of illness. I had the rare privilege of serving Bishop Jokomo as his conference secretary throughout his episcopacy from 1992 to 2004, with the exception of 1995–1996, when I was away for some studies. Hence, I can confidently speak about the amazing characteristics of his form and style of leadership.

Consequently, in 2004 the Zimbabwe Episcopal Area sent its delegates to the General Conference held in Pittsburg, Pennsylvania. I was elected the head of the delegation from the Zimbabwe East Annual Conference. Our bishop was not at the General Conference for obvious reasons. When we came back home, we began to hear gossip as it were that Zimbabwe might elect a new bishop to succeed Bishop Jokomo. Some of us who were at the General Conference did not take such talk seriously because at the time of celebrating the retiring bishops at that conference, the name of Bishop Jokomo was not called, nor did we expect his name to be on the list. Later on, we heard that a special conference was going to be called and that Bishop Machado of Mozambique was to preside at that special conference. Indeed, that special conference was held to nominate a slate of prospective candidates for the episcopacy. The Africa Central Conference was held in Johannesburg, South Africa, where I was elected bishop.

With how much joy does one receive such a package of grace, when you feel deep down that the opportunity has come not in a normal transition but because your predecessor became sick? Soon after my consecration, the other delegates and their bishops left. I remember very well that Bishop Muzorewa was the one who read the charge of episcopacy on me. But soon after that, I have no recollection of how and when the bishop left. I tagged on to the Zimbabwean delegation, who were not successful in hiding the feeling that they genuinely did not know how to relate to a person they had just raised from an ordinary pastor to the bishop of the church. Neither did I know how to behave in the midst of colleagues and companions in the church.

Upon returning to Zimbabwe, we went to the bishop's residence where we briefed Bishop Jokomo about the happenings at the Africa Central Conference. The bishop welcomed us and offered a prayer of thanksgiving for the gift of the bishop for the church. We then departed to our different places. I returned to Mutare and continued with my responsibilities at Africa University. I doubt very much whether students took me seriously in what I tried to lecture on and assign in classes. They knew very well that I was winding up. On September 1, newly elected bishops in The United Methodist Church, if they follow the connectional calendar, become effective in their respectively assigned areas. I went to the office in Mutare. The secretary did not know what to do with me. All she could say was that they were looking for a room that could be used as an office by the bishop. I returned home and worked from there, doing some planning and related matters. The issue of the office was revised within a relatively short time.

The other development was the most glaring one in showing that the episcopal area was taken by surprise in that indeed, they now had a new bishop for whom they must prepare. As it turned out, the episcopal area had no clear plans about where their new bishop was to stay. We continued to stay at our home in Mutare from September 2004 to February 2005. In the fourth month, the episcopacy committee had approached me saying that we could now move to Harare into a house temporarily for us. We could then move into the episcopal residence later on. It was one of the most difficult decisions I had to make in my experience as a bishop. My answer was no, but the issue of timing came into play. If I agreed to their arrangement I was going to put me and my family in a bind. What would happen if staying in that temporary house extended into a year or more? To push for a quick move could be easily be interpreted as my putting pressure on my predecessor to move out of the episcopal residence. I just did not like that idea. On the other hand, to say no then and there would have been taken as if I was being stubborn and antagonistic.

No bishop, at least in The United Methodist Church, wants to be viewed that way. I was clear in understanding that the leverage I had to push matters was if I continued to stay in our own house in Mutare. I told the committee that I was going to come back to them. On the other hand, I also knew that the leaders were doing their best in a difficult situation. I decided to just keep quiet hoping that they would have discerned on their own that I was not forthcoming on taking up their suggestion. Thank God the chair of the episcopacy committee did not follow up with me.

At the same time, some bishops at council meetings were beginning to ask me in passing about how the process of transition was moving on in the Zimbabwe Episcopal Area. I usually dodged the question and became evasive. I knew that they were somehow following events.

Sometime in February 2005 I received a call to say that we could then move to Harare on a specified date and that everything about transportation was in place. There was no prior consultation with me, so on the day the family moved to Harare, I was out in the country on church business. The rest is water under the bridge.

All these anomalies, small as they might look, would have been avoided were our transition not driven by circumstances beyond our control. Hence my clarion call at the 2016 Annual Conference in naming the quadrennium 2017–2020 as a transitional one. I knew what I was saying to the church. True to the topic, I can assert that the secret to ensuring a smooth transition for episcopal processes lies in thorough and transparent planning.

The Africa Central Conference in Luanda, Angola 2016

The Africa Central Conference took place in Angola, August 11–14. I was the president of the conference at that time. In my episcopal address to the conference, I spoke on "Planning for a New Dispensation as We Make Disciples for Jesus Christ in the Africa Central Conference." I intentionally primed the delegates to make some key decisions to reshape our central conference. I emphasized the good thing the conferences did in raising money for us to hold the central conference from our own coffers. We got help from the General Board of Global Ministries in the amount of twenty thousand dollars, but the bulk of the amount needed we raised ourselves. In my speech I pointed out that this was the right direction if the church was to be self-reliant in doing its ministries in Africa. I went on to use the words in the lyrics of the song that Oliver Mtukudzi, a Zimbabwean musician, used to sing. The opening line in Shona says, *"Remangwana raka jeka. Zuva kuzobuda handiti rinonga rambodoka".* The English translation is, "Tomorrow's future is bright. When the sun rises it would have set first."

I energized the Africa Central Conference by urging the delegates to know that "this session of the Central Conference is charged by a feeling of excitement as we celebrate and anticipate a hopeful future. It is a central conference session that should embrace lasting change for now and for the future generations. Those who will come after us should read about the work and decisions of this conference and nod their heads and say in the words of Sir Winston Churchill, 'This was their finest hour,' as leaders of the church."[13]

Major Changes for the Nomination of Episcopal Candidates

The Africa Central Conference passed a number of changes regarding the nomination and election of bishops. I shall focus on a selected few of those changes: (1) Ballot shall be used in nominating candidates. (2) The ballots are to be counted at the venue of the conference. (3) The top three are the duly nominated candidates. (4) The top three ballots should be sealed in an envelope. (5) The ballots should show statistical details, sealed, stamped, and signed by the presiding bishop and the secretary, and the certificates to be sent to the president of the college of bishops and the Africa Central Conference committee on episcopacy for verification before elections. (6) The nominated candidates should provide CV, which shall include pictures, historical background of the candidate, medical report, and other experiential documents verified by the annual conference Board of Ordained Ministry. (7) The top three are free to campaign after nominations. (8) "The office of the bishop shall not in any way or any [manner] be involved in campaigning for a candidate."[14] Let me make a disclaimer that this information is for the purpose of making a point in this book. This should not be used as the definitive product of all that the Africa Central Conference agreed on. It is the responsibility of each and every candidate to have access to the actual minutes of the Africa Central Conference of 2016 in Angola.

Retirement

Many societies and communities are still agrarian in their economies and do not understand retirement as many know it. I have witnessed my cousin continue working in his old age to the time of his death. This was work at his home with no pay from anywhere. Africans in the villages are still self-sufficient in many ways. They have a small field to grow crops and livestock to provide milk and meat. They sell some to get money to send the children to school or buy some items they could not make for themselves. Security for old age is built into these resources and from the children. So, retirement is not something talked about or on their agenda for daily discussion as families. In that sense, retirement is a foreign practice.

In his book, *Aging and Ministry in the 21st Century*, Richard Gentzler Jr. has delineated three phases of retirement. These are:

Active phase: The active phase is called the "Go-Go" phase. In this phase the older people might still pursue a number of productive activities. Some take up some employment full- or part-time.

Passive phase: This phase is called the "Slow-Go" phase. In this phase everything is sliding down to a reduced scale. Energy, mobility, and health will be ebbing. Activities are cut short in duration.

Final phase: This one is the "No-Go" phase. Health problems arise and it becomes impossible to do things and make movements that were simple before. In this phase, the older people are conscious of their impending death and prepare for it if the situation permits.[15]

My Own Retirement

I am not planning to reinvent the wheel for my retirement. I will follow best practices, which basically say one is better off if one keeps an active life. The advice is to disconnect yourself from work slowly, not in an abrupt manner. There are a lot of activities one can choose from: volunteering, learning a new skill as a hobby, reading. Reading is already my hobby. Exercising might be increased but always being mindful that it is within limits.

I will also get guidance from my personality. I don't live a restless type of life. Where possible, I want to determine the course of my life, especially how I will be in retirement. I favor doing some work, but not too much scheduling as if I were entering the job market for the first time.

For some time in my career, I have been entertaining a theory about retirement that I am not sure yet whether it works or not. I am convinced that in order to retire well you have to prepare for your retirement, following the best advice out there. On top of that, I believe in working hard, that is doing everything you might want to do while you are still doing the job. Get tired of doing all you wanted to do. You must get to the point of saying to yourself, "What is there which I have not done?" Understand me correctly: work will never be finished. But for my purposes, I want to reach a point of equilibrium in my thought about work. I want to be satisfied whenever I think of work. Retirement becomes a problem if the retiree is still yearning to still be doing the job she or he has retired from. I don't want that kind of retirement.

Conclusion

The chapter has focused on transition, as it relates to the experiences in the Zimbabwe Episcopal Area. The hope is that we will have a form of transition that will be smooth and joyous. Retirement is part of transition, and I wish it well for myself too.

As a word of gratitude, I thank the people of the Zimbabwe Episcopal Area for the blessed time we had together. I am thankful to God for walking with me through the journey of life to the present. This is indeed by the grace of God.

12

SEPARATION AND THE FUTURE OF THE UNITED METHODIST CHURCH IN AFRICA

Historical Background

The United Methodist Church has had a long history of divisions. The difference with what is happening today with the churches breaking away lies in the contending issues. In the nineteenth century the main cause of these divisions was slavery and the distribution of power between the episcopacy and the General Conference. There were those who did not see any incongruence with the issue of slavery while on the other hand preaching the good news. The power struggle was focused on the bishops. Some thought that the General Conference should be the ultimate body on decision-making and not the bishops. They viewed the bishops as the creation of the General Conference. The other side was for a strong episcopacy that should not be subservient to the General Conference.

Events of today are better understood if we have an understanding of the nature of those divisions. There are certain patterns the early divisions followed that are similar to what the church has been experiencing in our time.

A Series of Early Divisions

There was the case of Robert Strawbridge, who defied authorities by allowing the local preachers to administer the holy sacraments in the 1700s.[1] Another incident of dissent was the Fluvanna action of disobedience. On May 18, 1779, at a conference held at Fluvanna County, Virginia, a majority of preachers voted to do away with the restraining ruling, which John Wesley had instituted in guiding the churches. The preachers put in place a presbytery of four ministers. They were to ordain each other and then ordain the rest. Bishop Asbury acted fast in bringing the preachers back to order, and that served the church for the time.[2]

The O'Kelly Schism

The issue with James O'Kelly was that he wanted the preachers to appeal if they felt that an appointment by the bishop was against the wishes of the preacher. O'Kelly formulated a motion to that effect at a General Conference. The matter was debated at length. But when the vote was taken the motion was defeated. O'Kelly could not take it. He and his followers walked out of the conference.[3] If the motion had passed, it meant that the bishop's appointment was subject to appeal if the preacher had some complaints against that appointment. The bottom line is that the responsibility and authority of the bishop in making appointments for the good of the church would have been limited. O'Kelly went on to form his own denomination called the Republican Methodist Church.[4]

O'Kelly was viewed by many at the time as "a troublemaker bent on disrupting the unity of the church."[5] Bishop Francis Asbury wrote in a letter to Thomas Morrell that O'Kelly wanted nothing short of being a bishop himself.[6]

Hammett Case

William Hammett was ordained by Wesley and came to America for missionary work. He did his missionary work in South Carolina and proved to be an effective preacher. The people wanted Hammett to be appointed their pastor by popular acclamation. When that did not happen, Hammett broke away from the church and formed his denomination known as the Primitive Methodist Church.[7] Upon Hammett's death, his followers returned to the Methodist church, and the Primitive Methodist Church came to an end.

Orange Scott

Orange Scott and his followers withdrew from the Methodist Episcopal Church in 1843 to form the Wesleyan Church. Scott gave two reasons for withdrawing from the Methodist Episcopal Church. He said that the Methodist Episcopal Church was (1) a slave-holding church, and (2) its government was not scriptural. When Scott died, his followers went back to the Methodist Episcopal Church.[8]

Separation of 1844

The major split in the Methodist Episcopal Church came about in 1844. This one split the church between the North and the South regions of the United States. At the center of their contentious issues was the power of the episcopacy and that of the General Conference. The issue that power and authority was tested against was slavery. Highlighting those issues was the case of Bishop James Andrew. After the death of his first wife, Bishop Andrew married a second wife who owned slaves. The church regarded him as a "slave owner." A committee of nine was set to look into the ways and means of resolving the matter. When time came for the committee to report at the General Conference of 1844, they reported that they were unable to find a solution to the problem. Instead, they presented what they called the "plan of separation."[9] Discussions and alternative motions at the General Conference failed to resolve the issue.

The vote to stop Bishop Andrew from exercising episcopal duties prevailed. The separation of the Methodist Episcopal Church took place immediately along regional lines. The South argued that the General Conference had no right to dismiss the bishop. In that regard, the South was for a strong episcopacy. On the other hand, the North wanted a strong General Conference. Two new denominations came into existence: The Methodist Episcopal Church South and The Methodist Episcopal Church North.[10] Years of acrimonious relationship followed. The situation continued like that until the reunion of 1939. As we know, the spirit of oneness continued to grow in the church, leading to the formation of The United Methodist Church in 1968.

What Do We Discern?

These are complex issues that are not easily understood, let alone by an author like me who is an outsider to American issues. There are, however, some patterns that can be observed.

First, there was lack of patience in dealing with misunderstandings with the aim of reaching amicable solutions. Withdrawal was usually held in abeyance as an option to end the conflicts. In some cases, it appears as if the breakaway was already determined; what remained was to find a pretext to effect it.

Second, there was no spirit of compromise. It was like winning a case as the only way out. Conversing to reach some compromise was seen as a show of weakness.

Third, in some cases there were ulterior motives behind the breakaway. Some of the leading individuals in the narrative of the divisions became too ambitious and self-seeking.

Fourth, the sentiments of animosity between the South and the North in secular America filtered into the church. President Lincoln is noted to have said that if the Methodists cannot keep together, how can the nation manage?[11]

Fifth, the procedures and language used in those days is similar to what The United Methodist Church is going through now. Today we talk about the "Protocol of Separation and Reconciliation," and in 1844 they presented the "Plan of Separation to the General Conference." The difference is in the semantics, but the intent is similar.

Sixth, after the breakaway, the church failed and they usually came back to the mother church. This residual sense of belonging to each other was demonstrated first in the reunion of 1939 and later in the unity of 1968.

Proposal to Dissolve The United Methodist Church

There have been talk and attempts to dissolve The United Methodist Church before. In his book, *The Magnificent Obsession*, Bishop Cannon narrates these efforts at dissolving the church.

"Perhaps the most dangerous action taken by the 1996 General Conference was the adoption of the proposal from the Consultation on Church Union in which we are to amalgamate with other churches that compose the Consultation on Church Union."[12] The bishop went on to point out that the Confederation of Churches was to have "a new name and overall organization." Bishop Cannon did not think that such a plan was workable. "Witness what has happened in this regard in the Church of Canada and the newly reorganized Church of Christ Uniting in Australia," Cannon noted.[13]

Bishop Cannon went on to say that a parallel proposal was taking place in the Council of Ministries. The proposal was "to abandon entirely the present organization of The United Methodist Church and replace it with a so-called global church, organized to include the small central conferences overseas on a parity with the large jurisdictional conferences in the United States."[14]

Which Way for the African United Methodists?

Any reader of a book has the privilege of making his or her own conclusions. But for the Africans who belong to The United Methodist Church in Africa, this narrative should be a wake-up call. When we met in Freetown, Sierra Leone, as the College of African Bishops, we picked up that there was talk in the air about proposals to dissolve The United Methodist Church. That realization led us bishops to agree to put out a press release that was meant in part to address the issue of dissolving the church.[15]

Taking all these issues into consideration, my advice to the people called United Methodists in Africa is to stay put. We thank God that the leaders were inspired to give us a theme of the moment for the General Conference which is akin to saying "stay put": ". . . and Know that I Am God." There is no reason whatsoever for the Africans to be engulfed in these separations. From the look of it, there have been positions taken on the other side about these issues that Africans have no idea about. Let us stay in the denomination passed on to us by our forefathers and mothers, working hand in hand with missionaries as our precious heritage.

The issue of homosexuality, which is being waved in the face of Africans as a magic wand to explain why they should leave the United Methodist Church, can easily be resolved in Africa. What has been nagging our people in Africa is poverty, not homosexuality. Where in any African community has anyone heard a clarion call that the problem pestering them was homosexuality? What we hear as we supervise the church are calls for clean water, building of clinics, building churches, parsonages and hospitals, need for more schools, caring for the orphans and much more. I have been telling the Zimbabwean United Methodists that the issue of homosexuality is being used as propaganda, made to agitate the people to leave The United Methodist Church. What can only lead to the dissolution of The United Methodist Church in Africa is failure of leadership.

Africans still need ample time to discuss these issues from the grassroots to the top leadership. We are at critical moment in the history of the church that demands that we approach these challenges with uttermost wisdom. Any mistake might confuse our people and disorient them in a denomination that they have come to love so much.

Africa has a rich heritage concerning the whole world of Christianity beyond The United Methodist Church. That heritage is not fully understood and appreciated even in Africa itself. Let us have a little taste of it from Professor Thomas C. Oden. In his book *How Africa Shaped the Christian Mind: Rediscovering the African Seedbed of Western Christianity*, he says: "Christianity was present all up and down the Nile in the fifth, sixth and seventh centuries and continued there in unbreached continuity following the Arab conquest."[16] Oden went on to note, "Early Christianity tells an historical narrative that deeply involved Africa from the very beginning, from Joseph to Moses to the exodus to the flight of the holy family to Egypt to the Ethiopian eunuch. These are African events that define the whole subsequent narrative of salvation history in the Christian view."[17]

Add to this the notation that Christianity spread early from the Pentecost to Africa. "Christianity went immediately to Africa as soon as it was proclaimed in Pentecost. Recall where the Ethiopian eunuch was headed. It spread quickly. Like a prairie fire, into the known nations of the world the 40s, 50s, and 60s. In those early decades Africa was a prime target for Christian witness, since a large number of Diaspora Jews had been long settled there," noted Professor Oden.[18]

The future of Christianity in Africa is bright. "What is required for young Africans today is to dwell by grace in Africa, to inhabit it confidently, to live within the earliest Africa traditions of scriptural wisdom for a long period of time. Then God will give them the grace once again to grasp the unique divine purpose in African history, just as those Africans of the first centuries dwelled in it, lived in Christ the hope of glory and passed it along to Europe and the world."[19] Oden urged that if Africans were to pass on Christianity to their children, "they must have confidence that Christianity is trustworthy, that Christianity is true and truly African, and not fundamentally alien to the African spirit."[20]

I get puzzled when I hear some of the young African leaders claiming that they have finally discovered where traditional views about Christianity are propagated. If anything, Africa is the hub of the traditionalist views in the interpretation of the scripture, preaching, in the songs and set of beliefs regarding Christianity. Africans are as literal as anyone can imagine in the way they understand biblical stories. There is no need to look anywhere else if the issue is to search for traditional Christian views. Come to Africa and not the other way round.

Let me end by saying that change is coming, irrespective of which denomination you find yourself in—that includes those already in existence and those to come in the future. There will be no free lunch in any of them. So, what should Africans do? There is need for a mindset that will take us on the path of self-reliance with all the seriousness it deserves. The figures tell the story. Numbers of church members in The United Methodist Church are dwindling. The small numbers will follow the new denominations as well. So where is the money going to come from? It will come from Africa. You can notice that the big media houses of the world are paying attention to Africa in a way we have not witnessed before. Apart from having untapped minerals and other forms of wealth, Africa has a majority of young people among its population. People are the main resource needed by the church and by any other organization worth its name.

We need to teach our people the stewardship of giving. A lot of development is taking place in our United Methodist Church in Africa, funded by the African church members themselves. The signs for pivoting and beginning to contribute to the financial coffers of the church, in and outside Africa, are there. Allow me to give the example of Zimbabwe. As I write this chapter in June 2023, we have just dedicated a second head office for the Zimbabwe East Annual Conference on April 23, 2023, in Mutare. The first one was built in Harare for the Zimbabwe West Annual Conference. The same could be said for the other African Episcopal Areas of The United Methodist Church.

"Africans are not beggars . . . Africans like to do for themselves. The Church is for the most part self-supporting," noted Bishop James Mathews remarking on his experience in Zimbabwe.[21] The bishop went on, "A notable example is the Harvest Offering taken once a year, after harvest, and in addition to their regular offering from week to week. It is used to undergird the total program of the Church. If United Methodists in the United States were to share at the same rate, we would receive a total of about $50 million in one offering!" observed Bishop Mathews.[22]

Congregational worship is a key component of the work and ministry of the church. In my illustrations, I am using Zimbabwe as a microcosm of what goes on in the rest of Africa among the United Methodists in their own areas. Again, we turn to the observations of Bishop Mathews: "We were deeply impressed by the powerful services of worship. Everybody participated in a wholehearted way; One could say they put their whole being in their glorifying of God. The music, the singing, the drums, the rattles, and the swaying of bodies in rhythm were all like nothing we had ever experienced elsewhere in this degree of intensity."[23]

Bishop Mathews stated that they missed that type of worship when they returned home. "So it was that when we returned to the more sedate and formal public worship with which we had been familiar, we found something lacking. It was dull and lifeless by comparison. Animated Christian worship in Africa is a great gift of God."[24] On describing all-night prayer called *pungwe* in Zimbabwe, the bishop had this to say: "A *pungwe* is a kind of combination camp-meeting and watch-night service but with a peculiar African flavor. It is thoroughly indigenous, thoroughly Christian, thoroughly involving, and thoroughly effective."[25]

Conclusion

We have tried to focus on having the background to the issues of separation engulfing The United Methodist Church. That knowledge is vital in shedding light on some of the developments that we are witnessing today. Such information should nudge the African United Methodists to rethink our moves before we get entangled in issues that we don't understand. It is clear that the issue of homosexuality is used in Africa for propaganda purposes. We have confidence that we are able to resolve these challenges without leaving The United Methodist Church. Our long Christian heritage in terms of the place of Africa in the story of salvation is one of the reasons for us to stay put. Why should we disturb our people, whose worshipping style has been gloriously described by Bishop Mathews? Let us spare our people from pointing them to another denomination. In any case, the issue of homosexuality will not be resolved by this ongoing separation. It will be a festering issue in churches there in the United States for years to come. Joining another denomination in that environment is like jumping from a frying pan into the fire.

EPILOGUE

I feel encouraged that this modest contribution to the inspirational literature will be of help to many people who need this book. There is no one-size-fits-all model in life. But I share the belief that working hard and remaining focused is a tested and proven path to follow in one's life.

Further, I am strongly convinced that God intervened for the positive in my life. Milestones in my life as game changers happened by the grace of God and not much as a result of my effort.

Finally, the book has given some glimpses into the episcopacy, though it is from a small corner of Africa, Zimbabwe. I have also attempted to share some of the best practices, which I tested in the field as I led the church in the Zimbabwe Episcopal Area of The United Methodist Church.

NOTES

Acknowledgments
1. E. K. Nhiwatiwa, "Preaching as God's Mission: A Commentary," in *Preaching as God's Mission*, ed. Tsuneaki Kato, Studio Homiletica 2 (Tokyo, Japan: Kyo BunKwan, Inc., 1999), 35–36.
2. E. K. Nhiwatiwa. "Preaching Task in Zimbabwe" in *Preaching as God's Mission*, ed. Tsuneaki Kato, Studio Homiletica 2 (Tokyo, Japan: Kyo BunKwan, Inc., 1999), 154–57.
3. For those who were elected to serve on the board, see Judith M. McDaniel, "Reflection on the Kyoto Conferences of Societas Homiletica and the Future" in *Preaching as God's Mission*, ed. Tsuneaki Kato, Studio Homiletica 2 (Tokyo, Japan: Kyo BunKwan, Inc., 1999), 2.

1. A Village Comes of Age
1. Misheck Samanyanga, "The Humba Clan," August 2019 https://www.blog.zimtribes.com/the-humba-clan
2. My sister passed on while I was still writing this book. May her soul rest in peace.
3. Mathias Mungwambi, my new friend with whom I acted as self-made comedian, also passed while this book was in the making.

2. Educational Odyssey
1. William Ragsdale Cannon, *A Magnificent Obsession: The Autobiography of William Ragsdale Cannon* (Nashville: Abingdon Press, 1999), 71–78.

3. My Faith Journey
1. Old Mutare Mission is where Methodism started in the Zimbabwe Episcopal Area.
2. Early morning prayers instilled the discipline of prayer in me.

4. In America
1. I orient relatives and friends who might be going to America for the first time.

5. Africa University Was My Crucible
1. Warren G. Bennis and Robert J. Thomas, "Crucibles of Leadership," in *On Mental Toughness* (*Harvard Business Review*, 2018), 11–12.

6. We Have an Election
1. William Ragsdale Cannon, *A Magnificent Obsession, The Autobiography of William Ragsdale Cannon* (Nashville: Abingdon Press), 182.
2. Bishop Earl Hunt, Jr., quoted in James C. Logan, *A Charge to Keep: The Life of Earl Gladstone Hunt, Jr.* (Nashville: Abingdon Press, 2000).
3. Cannon, *A Magnificent Obsession*, 183.
4. Sharon Zimmerman Rader and Margaret Ann Crain. *Women Bishops of the United Methodist Church: Extraordinary Gifts of the Spirit* (Nashville: Abingdon Press, 2019), 69.
5. Ibid.
6. Ibid.

7. Cannon, *A Magnificent Obsession*, 182.
8. Ibid., 196.
9. Ibid.

7. My Episcopacy

1. James K. Mathews, *Set Apart to Serve: The Role of the Episcopacy in the Wesleyan Tradition* (Nashville: Abingdon Press, 1985), 13.
2. Ibid., 25.
3. Ibid., 238–40.
4. William H. Willimon, *Bishop: The Art of Questioning Authority by an Authority in Question* (Nashville: Abingdon Press, 2012). I found the chapter on leading change helpful for me, pp. 65–88.
5. Jeanette Marais, "Give Yourself Permission to be Successful" in *The Book Every Leader Needs to Read: Lessons from Leading Business Minds and Thought Leaders* (Bryanston, South Africa: Tracey McDonald Publishers, 2021), 132.
6. Chenayi Kumuterera, "Bishop Nhiwatiwa Earns Many Nicknames," United Methodist News Weekly Digest, 2018.
7. Ibid.
8. Ibid.
9. Ibid.
10. Jack M. Tuell, *The Organization of The United Methodist Church, 2005–2008 Edition* (Nashville: Abingdon Press, 2005), 107.
11. Ibid.

8. Chabadza Partnerships

1. Annual reports and work plans from CHABADZA Competence Seminar, Oslo, Norway, 14th–22nd September 2015, p.14. Gelly Miti, the Finance Officer at the Chabadza Office in Mutare, Zimbabwe, gave the cited report in Oslo, Norway in September 2015. All the Chabadza documents are in one file labeled "Annual Reports and Work Plans, CHABADZA."

Citation for this chapter hereafter will be "Chabadza File," followed by relevant detail of the source and content.
2. Chabadza File, Competence Report Workshop 2013, 10.
3. Ibid.
4. Chabadza File, Community Development Programme, Annual Narrative Report, 2018, 9.
5. Chabadza File, Annual Narrative Report, 2016, 1.
6. Ibid.
7. Chabadza File, Quarterly Narrative Report, 2016, 3.
8. Chabadza File, Competence Workshop, 2013, 11. Torill Langbraathen, who gave the cited remarks, was the chairperson of the Board of Global Ministries of Norway.
9. Chabadza File, Competence Workshop, 2010, 40. The workshop was still at the policy-making stage and was held in Harare, Zimbabwe.
10. Ibid.
11. Chabadza File, Narrative Report 2021, 10.
12. Chabadza File, Educational Project Building a Better Tomorrow at Chikwizo in the Mudzi District. A pamphlet on the project is enclosed in the file.
13. Chabadza File, Pamphlet on a dip tank project in Nyamacheni Gokwe.
14. Chabadza File, Pamphlet on the Waiting Mother's Shelter at the Nyamombe Clinic in the Mutasa Nyanga District.
15. Chabadza File, Pamphlet on the Chitora Bridge in the Mutare District.

9. Mukati Council of Bishops
1. William B. Oden and Robert J. Williams, *The Council of Bishops in Historical Perspective: Celebrating 75 Years of the Life and Leadership of the Council of Bishops of the United Methodist Church* (Nashville: Abingdon Press, 2014), 25.

2. Ibid., 43–44.
3. James K. Mathews, *Set Apart to Serve: The Role of the Episcopacy in the Wesleyan Tradition* (Nashville: Abingdon Press, 1985), 227.
4. Oden and Williams, *The Council of Bishops in Historical Perspective*, xii.
5. Ibid., 244.
6. Mathews, *Set Apart*, 258.
7. Oden and Williams, *The Council of Bishops in Historical Perspective*, 17.
8. Ibid., 295.

10. Leadership: A Repertoire of Skills

1. Ronald Heifetz, Alexander Grashow, and Marty Linsky, *The Practice of Adaptive Leadership: Tools and Tactics for Changing Your Organization and the World* (Boston: Harvard Business Press, 2009), 32.
2. Ibid.
3. James K. Mathews and William B. Oden, eds., *Vision and Supervision: A Sourcebook of Significant Documents of The Council of Bishops of The United Methodist Church, 1968–2002*. With a preface by Bishop Sharon A. Brown Christopher, president of the Council of Bishops (Nashville: Abingdon Press, 2003), 9.
4. *The Book of Discipline of The United Methodist Church*, 1980. Copyright 1980 by The United Methodist Publishing House; para. 501.
5. Ibid., para. 502.
6. Ibid.
7. Ibid.
8. Ibid., para. 137.
9. Brian Tracy, *Eat That Frog!: 21 Great Ways to Stop Procrastinating and Get More Done in Less Time,* (Oakland: Berrett-Koehler Publishers, 2017), 13.

10. Ibid.
11. Daniel Goleman, "What Makes a Leader?" in *HBR at 100* (Boston: Harvard Business Review Press, 2022), 21–41.
12. Tracy, *Eat That Frog!*, 105.
13. Ibid.
14. Simon Sebag Montefiore, intro, *Speeches that Changed the World* (London: Smith-Davies Publishers, 2005), 69.
15. Sam Silverstein, *No More Excuses! The Five Accountabilities for Personal and Organizational Growth* (Shippensburg, PA: Sound Wisdom, 2015,), 46
16. Tracy, *Eat That Frog!*, 25.
17. Tony Schwartz, author of *Be Excellent at Anything: The Four Keys to Transforming the Way We Work and Live*, as quoted in Amy Gallo, "How to Build Confidence: Become More Self-Assured at Work," in *Confidence*, Emotional Intelligence Series (Boston: Harvard Business Review Press, 2019), 4.
18. Rosabeth Moss Kanter, "Overcome the Eight Barriers to Confidence," in ibid., 18–22.
19. Michael Heath, *Leadership Secrets* (London: HarperCollins, 2010), 96.
20. Sharon Zimmerman Rader and Margaret Ann Crain, *Women Bishops of the United Methodist Church: Extraordinary Gifts of the Spirit* (Nashville: Abingdon Press, 2019), 126–27.
21. Ibid., 127.
22. Judith Craig, *The Leading Women: Stories of the First Women Bishops of The United Methodist Church* (Nashville: Abingdon Press, 2004,) 260.
23. Roderick Gilkey and Clint Kilts, "Cognitive Fitness" in *HBR's 10 Must Reads on Mental Toughness* (Boston: Harvard Review Press, 2018), 42–43.
24. Ibid., 43

25. Warren G. Bennis and Robert J. Thomas, "Crucibles of Leadership" in *HBR's 10 Must Reads on Mental Toughness*, (Boston: Harvard Business Review Press, 2018), 23.
26. Alia Crum and Thomas Crum, "Stress Can Be a Good Thing If You Know How to Use It" in *HBR's 10 Must Reads on Mental Toughness*, (Boston: Harvard Business Review Press, 2018), 71–75.
27. Ibid., 74.
28. Silverstein, *No More Excuses!*, 40.
29. Ibid., 36.
30. Tracy, *Eat that Frog!*, 25.
31. Ibid., 31.
32. Silverstein, *No More Excuses!*, 51.
33. Ibid.
34. Adriaan Groenewald, *"What's Missing in the World of Leadership?*" MCA Training International website, February 17, 2021. https://www.mcatraininginternational.com/whats-missing-in-the-world-of-leadership/.

11. Transition and Retirement

1. Myles Munroe, *The Principles and Benefits of Change: Fulfilling Your Purpose in Unsettled Times*, (New Kensington, PA: Whitaker House, 2009), 7.
2. Ibid.
3. Ibid.
4. Komal Gulati, "How to navigate successful leadership transitions" (June 24, 2022). Internet source: https://www.td.org/atd-blog/how-to-navigate-successful-leadership-transitions.
5. Ibid.
6. Africa Central Conference, Luanda, Angola, 11–14 August, 2016, *Official Journal, The Zimbabwe East Annual Conference of the United Methodist Church*, 327–42.

7. Ralph E. Dodge, *The Revolutionary Bishop Who Saw God at Work in Africa* (Pasadena: William Carey Library, 1986), 169.
8. Ibid.
9. Abel Tendekayi Muzorewa, *Rise Up and Walk: An Autobiography* (Nashville: Abingdon Press, 1978), 65.
10. Ibid.
11. Dodge, *The Revolutionary Bishop*, 169.
12. Ibid.
13. Churchill said in a memorable speech about the British armed forces in June 18, 1950, to the House of Commons of the UK that "This was their finest hour."
14. Zimbabwe East Conference. Central Conference Report, 2016.
15. Richard H. Gentzler. Jr. *Aging and Ministry in the 21st Century: An Inquiry Approach* (Nashville: Discipleship Resources, 2008), 41.

12. Separation and the Future of The United Methodist Church in Africa

1. James K. Mathews, *Set Apart to Serve: The Role of the Episcopacy in the Wesleyan Tradition* (Nashville: Abingdon Press, 1985), 78–79.
2. Ibid, 80.
3. Ibid., 140–41.
4. Ibid.
5. Ibid.
6. Ibid., 141.
7. Ibid.
8. William B. Oden and Robert J. Williams, *The Council of Bishops in Historical Perspective: Celebrating 75 Years of the Life and Leadership of the Council of Bishops of the United Methodist Church* (Nashville: Abingdon Press, 2014), 21.
9. Ibid.

10. Ibid.
11. Ibid., 31. The authors noted that if the Methodists became reconciliatory as expressed in President Lincoln's Second Inauguration speech, there would have been peace among them.
12. William Ragsdale Cannon, *A Magnificent Obsession: The Autobiography of William Ragsdale Cannon* (Nashville: Abingdon Press, 1999), 358.
13. Ibid.
14. Ibid., 358–59.
15. Press release at College of the African Bishops in Freetown, Sierra Leone.
16. Thomas C. Oden, *How Africa Shaped the Christian Mind: Rediscovering the Seedbed of Western Christianity* (Downers Grove, IL: InterVarsity Press, 2007), 84.
17. Ibid., 96-97.
18. Ibid., 125.
19. Ibid., 105.
20. Ibid.
21. James K. Mathews, *A Global Odyssey: The Autobiography of James K. Mathews* (Nashville: Abingdon Press, 2000), 469.
22. Ibid.
23. Ibid., 468.
24. Ibid.
25. Ibid.